Praise for Steve Suggs and **can|they|sell**

*To hire or not to hire? That is the question... Steve Suggs'
book -* Can They Sell *is THE answer! Every sales manager
faces the dilemma, should I or shouldn't I hire this candidate? Will this person be a winner or a whiner? Steve Suggs
provides wisdom and insight that will lead you to the BEST
answer. If you're looking to turn a new hire into a sales
superstar, buy this book today."*

Jeffrey Gitomer, *author of* **The Little Book of Leadership** *and the*
Sales Bible

*Fully 90% of your success as a sales manager or business
owner is determined by the quality of salespeople you have.
This book shows you how to take the guess work out of
recruiting top performers.*

Brian Tracy, *Author, The Psychology of Selling*
www.BrianTracy.com

*When I am hired to train a sales force the first thing that
becomes obvious to me is how well the hiring decisions were
made. Some people will sell and some won't...no matter how
much you train them. Question number one must be, "Can
They Sell?" and there are ways to know the answer to this
before you hire them. Steve Suggs has done us all a great
favor by writing this insightful book. Now we have a guide to
make much better decisions and to start people on a path that
they too will find satisfying.*

Jim Cathcart, *author of* Relationship Selling, *Hall of Fame*
Speaker http://Cathcart.com

I would sincerely recommend Can They Sell *as the single best "How To" book on recruiting and selecting salespeople that I have ever read. While there are many other resources in this area, this particular book is the only one that I have found that combines recent research, best practices, personal experience, and step-by-step recommendations by an authority who has "been there and done it." I especially appreciated access to the forms and questionnaires which are used in every step of the process. I consider it a "must read" for anyone in sales management who wants to hire peak performing salespersons.*

Dr. Larry L. Craft, *CEO, SalesPower Roundtable™*

Recruiting salespeople is the hardest part of a sales manager's job. The wrong decision can cost you thousands. Read Can They Sell *and you'll discover where to find quality candidates, what to look for in them, and how to look for it. Get it, read it and use it to start recruiting sales superstars.*

Dr. Tony Alessandra, *author of* **Collaborative Selling** *and* **The Platinum Rule for Sales Mastery** *www.Alessandra.com*

In today's business environment, your salespeople are your primary differentiator. To get the best ones, you need to stop trusting your gut and read Can They Sell.

Jill Konrath, *author of* **SNAP Selling** *and* **Selling to Big Companies** *www.JillKonrath.com*

Steve Suggs nails it! Finally there is a book that teaches you how to do it right. Can They Sell *gives you access to a comprehensive sales recruiting system that really works. Read the book, use the tools and there are no more excuses for the bad hiring decisions that cost you thousands.*

Jeb Blount, *Author of* **People Follow You** *and founder of Sales-Gravy.com*

Executives develop strategic plans of grandeur which fall flat when the sales people can't execute them. These executives quickly come to find that they don't have the right sales people on the team to do the things that need to be done. In Can They Sell, *Steve Suggs provides executives with an actionable toolkit empowering them to make informed decisions in the hiring process. Read this book and put the methodology into practice!*

Lee B. Salz, *Sales Management Strategist and Award Winning Author, SalesArchitects.com*

Whether starting out fresh or inheriting a sales team, this is your INSIGHT book. Through stories of experience, statistics and simple examples, Steve demonstrates the art of recruiting. Within these pages are the secrets to what I hear Sales Managers asking all the time: What exactly is the "Best Salesperson Profile"? How do you use Science to measure Personality Traits? And, can you discover hidden character flaws when screening resumes? No longer does hiring a good salesperson have to be a "roll of the dice."

Terri Dunevant, *Award-winning Author,* **The Staircase Principle**

You need a recruiting system—Steve Suggs, in Can They Sell, *tells you how to find and hire the right salespeople. When you select the best, they are successful and don't leave. That equals high growth and makes you a hero. Learn what this book has to teach, and you will have a strong foundation of a great recruiter and sales coach.*

Randy Schwantz, *Author of* **How to Get Your Competition Fired Without Saying Anything Bad About Them,** *www.thewedge.net*

Sales managers need a system for finding the best sales-people. If you're just looking for a "warm body" to fill a sales position, don't read this book. But if you want to lead a sales force instead of a sales department, make sure you understand and implement the system Steve Suggs lays out in Can They Sell.

Chris Lytle, *author of* **The Accidental Sales Manager** *and* **The Accidental Salesperson**

"Why can't we find any good salespeople!" thus goes the rant in so many companies, maybe even yours? If so Steve Suggs has put together the next best thing to cloning. Can They Sell *gives you the systems that sort, clarify and sepa-rate the true winners for you. How do you pick, much less determine, if the sales candidate has the right behaviors? right attitude? right drive?* Can They Sell *gives you the systems, process and answers to make your next hire the right one. Not reading this book can be costly to you and your business!*

Harlan Goerger, *President AskHG, 3 time Business Author, Trainer, Consultant*

You like them, but ...

can|they|sell

Learn to
RECRUIT THE BEST
Salespeople

Steve Suggs

Vision Run Publishing
Knoxville, TN
2012

Can They Sell
Learn to Recruit the Best Salespeople

For permissions contact:
Steve Suggs 865-567-2871
ssuggs@salesmanage.com

Recruit the Best © by Sales Manage Solutions, LLC. Used by permission. All rights reserved.

Craft Personality Questionnaire © and *(CPQ)* © by SHL Group Ltd. Used by permission. All rights reserved.

Book jacket design: Haley Dotson and Steve Suggs
Logo design: Forty-seven Media
Authors photo: Lorelei Bryan GentleTouchPortraits.com

Printed in the United States.

www.VisionRun.com

For my family
Tammy, Clint, Haley, Michael and Gail –
the family for whom I do my best every day

Thank you God for all blessings!

A special thank you to Lance Cooper, my phenomenal
business partner – without him, this book would have
been impossible

Thank you Gail Pigg and Debbie Patrick –
your writing and editing skills are invaluable

Learn to RECRUIT THE BEST Salespeople

Steve Suggs

We are hardwired by genetics, but shaped by our environment. This fact has always fascinated me. It is often framed as a "nature versus nurture" debate, but after years of study and practical application, I have discovered a "best practice" recruiting system that answers the question, "CAN THEY SELL?"

Part One

"Recruit the Best" System –
Knowledge, Tools and Skills Inside a Process

"After many failed attempts to get sparkling people to survive in a high-rejection, high-activity sales career, it occurred to me that recruiting is much more complicated. The best salespeople are multi-dimensional. To be successful as a sales leader, I needed to find out what these dimensions were and figure out how to measure them in each candidate."

*"The NFL has a system that begins with a profile
of the perfect NFL player, and every 'wannabe' is
compared against that profile. They know how tall,
how smart, how strong, how proficient—everything.
It is no Little League game. These guys are in it to
win, to get the best in the nation, or even the world
and nothing less will do. This is the kind of sales
coach you want to be, and the type of team you want
to recruit."*

Chapter 3:

*These four key elements in the "Recruit the Best system
help you answer the questions, "WHAT traits do I
look for?" and "HOW do I look for these traits?"*

1) The "Best Salesperson Profile"
*2) A process to follow, including step-by-step
directions from initial contact to hire*
*3) Tools to use - structured questionnaires,
assessments, and scoring/matching sheets*
*4) Skills in interviewing, screening, and the
discipline to follow the system*

*The "Recruit the Best" system contains three stages
- Screening, Profiling and Interviewing. Using the
selection tools in each stage helps make a considered, logical decision rather than a quick, emotional
decision.*

This is a very important chapter. The "Recruit the Best" system taught in this book is unique and different because it uses the combination of character and personality to predict a salesperson's level of sales success. This knowledge of trait-combination and the tools to measure for the traits are explained in this chapter.

Now that you have a more comprehensive understanding of what to look for while selecting salespeople, these tips will make the boring job of screening resumes much easier. Other ways to use the resume throughout the recruiting process to discover hidden character flaws are revealed in these tips.

Great sales leaders do their best every day for the benefit of others.

Introduction

Recruiting and Retaining the Best Salespeople Requires a "Best Practice" Recruiting System

We are hardwired by genetics, but shaped by our environment. This fact has always fascinated me. It is often framed as a "nature versus nurture" debate, but after years of study and practical application, I have discovered a "best practice" recruiting system that answers the question, "Can They Sell?"

For those of us who manage salespeople, either as sales leaders or business owners, the task of recruiting and retaining top performing salespeople is daunting. We have to recruit, train, coach and inspire sales teams in the face of overwhelming cultural, competitive and technological challenges. Like every other area of business, we are challenged to produce more efficiently and more reliably than ever before. That means we cannot afford to make mistakes.

As a salesperson, success is dependent primarily upon individual effort. As a sales leader, success is dependent upon your efforts as a sales leader as well as the efforts of those whom you choose for your sales team. Recruiting decisions impact you personally as well as those you recruit. So how do you go about making critical recruiting decision?

When I ask sales leaders, "What is the hardest part of your job?", they always tell me, "Recruiting and retaining salespeople." When I ask them to describe the traits they are looking for and the process they use to look for these traits, I almost never get an answer which shows that they have a clear understanding of a "best practice" recruiting system. Many of these same sales leaders can clearly articulate the face-to-face sales system they use to sell their product. They can also tell me about the system they use to plan their sales strategies and sales productivity. So why do they not have a similar system for recruiting salespeople?

I have discovered the primary reason that most sales leaders do not have a system for recruiting is because there are very few comprehensive recruiting resources available. Many resources approach recruiting with a focus on a single piece of the large puzzle of recruiting. There are many resources that provide interview questions; and others that teach interviewing techniques; and still others that focus on using a personality assessment as the primary decision tool. All of these resources are helpful; however, they are not part of a comprehensive system that measures specific character traits and personality traits that determine salespeople's ability to master sales skills.

> This book is unique because of the knowledge of human behavior that is taught inside the recruiting system. This same knowledge, used in recruiting, becomes the foundation for coaching the members of your sales team.

I chose to write this book because I wanted to give sales leaders a resource that covers all areas of the recruiting process. This book contains a "best practice" recruiting system with the knowledge, tools and skills needed to recruit and retain the best salespeople. This book is unique because of the knowledge of human behavior that is taught inside the recruiting system. This same knowledge, used in recruiting, becomes the foundation for coaching the members of your sales team.

Following a "best practice" recruiting system is critical to having a strong business in the new economy. As sales cycles are shortened, competition increases, and markets are sluggish, finding and keeping a top performing sales team is now more important, and more difficult, than ever before.

The most complex problems have always been solved with systems and processes.

There is so much overlooked power in systems. The reason cars became so luxurious and affordable is that Henry Ford created a system for mass production. For almost one hundred years, all car manufacturers have mastered a reliable production system that sources parts, labor and manufacturing.

The housing and building trade has also benefitted from systems. Since the housing boom that started at the end of World War II, builders and architects have used ever-improving systems to design and construct strong and efficient buildings at a reasonable price. These systems have empowered the American dream.

We have the science, the patterns of success, and methodology to create a best-practices system for recruiting and coaching salespeople.

Similarly, since the mid-1950's psychologists have been studying human dynamics. We now have systems of acquiring and analyzing the information about human behavior that we need in order to make great hiring decisions. All the raw materials are available. We have the science, the patterns of success, and methodology to create a best-practices system for recruiting and coaching salespeople.

More than ever in America today, to have a strong business, we must master these major business processes:

- Define the benefits and features of our product or service and how our offerings are different from the competition.

- Develop sales and marketing skills and strategies that create customers, keep customers, and gain market share.

- Build human capital for strong sales and service cultures.

All these business processes must be present and working in concert if we are to survive in a struggling economy, a changing culture, and the resulting competitive environment. Just as we have mastered the benefits and features of our product, just as we have mastered the steps in a best-practice face-to-face sales process, so we must master the steps in a best-practice recruiting and coaching system in order to select and retain top salespeople.

The best-practice recruiting system we have created at Sales Manage Solutions is called the "Recruit the Best" system.

The elements of the "Recruit the Best" system are WHERE, WHAT and HOW.

- Knowing WHERE to find enough quality candidates to interview.

- Knowing WHAT to look for in the best salespeople.

- Knowing HOW to use processes, tools and skills to look for the sales-specific traits and skills.

Why is it so hard to recruit salespeople?

Whether the economy is thriving or thrashing, good sales-people are hard to find. One candidate after another will tell you, "I am a people person," as if that alone is enough. It is not. The primary reason recruiting salespeople is so hard is this fact: people are complicated - extremely complicated.

It becomes easier to agree with the fact that people are com-plicated when you consider the changing landscape of our culture. A study by the Hoover Institute, a part of Stanford University, tells us that the past twenty-five years have seen unprecedented change, beginning with the family unit. "The traditional American Family has been undergoing profound transformations for all ages, all races, and all ethnic groups," the study said. "These include the number of adults who marry, the number of house-holds that are formed by married people, the number of children that are conceived, the economic role of mothers, the number of non-family households, and even the importance of marriage in accounting for total births."

Add to the changing family dynamics the increasing cultural and religious diversity, and you can begin to see how the markets to which you sell are changing demographically, as are the pools of candidates when looking for salespeople. By the time young people finish high school they have been exposed to fifty different teachers, all with different beliefs and values. With the completion of a four-year college degree, you can add another forty to that number.

The average young person does not leave home, the classic sign of adulthood, until the age of 26. Some would call that "Fail-ure to Launch" except that it is no longer a funny movie with a cool Matthew McConaughey as the star. It is a frustrating reality for many parents and employers. According to *Psychology Today,* the number of adults aged 25-34 still living at home is up 20% since 1982.

One of the explanations as to why it is so hard to find good salespeople is outlined in Michael Kimmel's book *Guyland: The Perilous World Where Boys Become Men.* He discusses the social evolution that has enabled young men to postpone growing up almost indefinitely. Our society has begun to condone a lifestyle that glorifies "guys" living in a state of youth-oriented suspended animation until age 30 and beyond, as they live together in an adult version of a college style frat house with no commitments, few responsibilities and almost no sense of direction. Their lives are largely centered around sports, women, parties and activities not fit for family viewing. There are twenty million males in this age bracket. This is not a good formula for society or for the career drive required for successful salespeople.

All this is, of course, in addition to the fact that technology has opened up new markets and completely transformed the way business is conducted. At the beginning of my career in the early 1980's we knew nothing of the Internet, emails or Facebook. To quote songwriter/poet Bob Dylan, "The times they are a-changin'."

Be Encouraged

I would be lying if I told you that learning to use the "Recruit the Best" system is simple. Once you learn the knowledge of human behavior taught in this book and learn to use the tools inside the system, recruiting gets much easier; however, because of the reasons mentioned above, selecting the best from the rest will always be complicated. If you decide to invest the time to master this system, you will have acquired a critical leadership skill that will be useful for the rest of your career and will almost certainly make your career more lucrative.

As we proceed, I want to give you this encouragement that will be helpful as you learn to put these processes into practice. I would like to begin with asking you not to give into the temptation to discredit the validity of this information and look for reasons this system will not work for you. Doubting the validity of a best-practice system is the perfect excuse to continue on the same ineffective path, expecting different results. It is like overweight people who say they have tried diet and exercise, but it just did not work for them. It is important to realize that it is usually not the system, but the person using the system that creates success or failure.

You may be using one or more of these common approaches to recruiting salespeople:

- Reviewing resumes, unstructured interviews and reference checks. (Many studies show this approach gives only 6% of the information needed to make a good hire.)

- Using interview questions not tied to specific character and Personality Traits.

- Using a personality assessment as the primary source of information to make a hiring decision. Only 20-30% of the information needed is found from this source; even though the assessment used is one of the most high-powered assessments.

- Spending time with the candidate and using gut and intuition to form an opinion as to whether or not the candidate is likable. If the candidate is likable, the interviewer transitions from selecting to selling the candidate on taking the job.

These approaches to recruiting are only pieces of a system. Without a system, emotions override logic. Without a system, recruiting is little more than a Las Vegas gamble. So it is no wonder why it seems hard to recruit people who can sell.

If you are a small business owner, and you make a great hiring decision, you most likely will not have to hire more than one to three people every year or so. This infrequent need to recruit leaves room for recruiting skills to get rusty. Mastering the use of tools and skills inside a best-practice recruiting system makes it easier to remember the skills that worked well during the last hire.

This book is about a system for recruiting salespeople, tied to the knowledge of human behavior. You will find a process with tools and skills needed for selecting the best from the rest. You will learn WHERE to look, WHAT to look for and HOW to look for it. Let's get started.

Part I:

"Recruit the Best" System – Knowledge, Tools and Skills Inside a Process

Chapter 1:

What the Heck is "Sparkle"?

Too often, sales training goes something like this: The sales manager takes the new salesperson on a call, the sales manager conducts the entire interview, and as they go back out to the car, he says to the salesperson, "There, that's how it's done."

It is impossible to know how much the sales associate learned, or did not learn. That is why you, as a sales manager, go along on the call. Watch the salesperson. Let the salesperson make the sale, or fail. Do not rescue him or her. Be sure you debrief afterwards. Otherwise, it is somewhat akin to a baseball batting coach teaching someone how to hit by batting and saying, "Watch how I do it." That is just not nearly enough. As a new sales manager, your training about recruiting may have been exactly like this sales manager.

You probably watched your boss conduct an interview, and were then told, "Go do it like I just did." Or your boss may have just said, "You have been through an interview before—get to it." That is what happened to me. My first training about recruiting was watching my boss do an interview. After the interviewee left, he said, "That is how we do it. Here's what we are looking for. The first thing we are looking for is sparkle."

I was thinking to myself, what the heck is sparkle? This kind of vague direction results in the fact that most people spend more time and effort buying a car or even a copy machine than they do in hiring a new salesperson *because they do not know how to do the right research and due diligence for finding and hiring the best salespeople.*

> **The best salespeople are multi-dimensional. To be successful as a sales leader, I needed to find out what these dimensions were and figure out how to measure them in each candidate.**

Is "sparkle" the main ingredient in the best salespeople? Are there not other important characteristics? What if these sparkling people are not honest? What if they are charismatic while presenting, but they do not have the work ethic to make enough presentations? After many failed attempts to get sparkling people to survive in a high-rejection, high-activity sales career, it occurred to me that recruiting is much more complicated than this. The best salespeople are multi-dimensional. To be successful as a sales leader, I needed to find out what these dimensions were and figure out how to measure them in each candidate.

This book will help you find some of the answers. It will get you solidly on the road to knowing where to find the best salespeople, what (specifically) to look for, and how to filter out those with merely sparkle in an interview from those who can actually sell.

Are the best salespeople an endangered species?

Great salespeople may seem to be an endangered species, but it is not because there are fewer of them. The changing times we live in have made it all but impossible for mediocre salespeople to survive. Today you <u>must</u> find and nurture great salespeople if you want your company to prosper, because the challenges are growing immensely.

It has never been easier for consumers to price shop, and a bad economy is making it essential for them to do so. On the Internet, they can buy online and bypass the personal sales staff altogether. The competition, no matter what your industry, is getting more aggressive with pricing gimmicks, strong advertising spin and branding campaigns, and constant innovations.

Consumers are more educated, more diverse demographically, and more price sensitive than ever before. For most industries, their target audience is aging because America is aging as a nation. The size of the senior population, those 65+, is expected to double in the next 25 years as the boomer generation ages. In the past, mass media and advertisers have typically targeted the age groups of either 18-49 or 25-54 year-olds. With the aging population, these typical demographic segments will be a smaller portion of the population as a whole, and in an effort to maintain audience numbers, media habits and offerings will naturally shift.

Sales managers, of course, realize the pressure to hire well. So they do what they do best: they start selling. They sell job candidates on the company, the product or services, and the benefit package. *That is the first mistake.*

What causes us to like the candidates?

Let me tell you a true story which, for me, was very illuminating. I was at a dinner club with my wife, seated at a table with a couple we had not met before. My wife does not like to talk much, and does not like it when I talk too much, so I decided to try an experiment. I kept asking open-ended questions, encouraging this couple to talk about themselves. I began with "Where are you from?" And followed up with, "Really? What was that like?" This was enough to keep them going, and talking throughout the entire evening. By the end of the evening, they commented on how much they liked us, and felt sure they had met us before. They warmly talked about how close they felt to us, and enjoyed getting to know us.

I was confused as to why they thought they knew us, when in fact that did not know anything about us. They did not ask us anything. With my prompting, they had talked about themselves all evening long. After reflecting on this story, I realized there is an important lesson here for sales managers. The unfortunate reality about human behavior is that the more we talk about ourselves the more we like the people to whom we are talking. We do not have to sell the candidates on our company as much as we might think. The more we let them talk, the more they like our company and want to work for us. Conversely, the more we talk about ourselves and our company to the candidates, the more we like the candidates, and want them to work for us, whether they really should or not.

As much as we all love to talk about our company, and as desperately as we may feel we need salespeople, we should guard against doing most of the talking in a job interview, and focus on the candidates. If we know what to look for, and which questions to ask, the candidates will eventually tell us everything we need to know.

Let us back up a moment and talk about the cost of getting it wrong. You are not hiring a salesperson, you are making a $100,000+ decision for the company. This is not an exaggeration. Use the worksheet below to find your personalized estimated cost of making a poor hiring decision. This is an eye-opening exercise.

The true cost of poor recruiting decisions can be difficult to measure in hard dollars, but this worksheet will give you a way to quantify the lost time, effort and dollars spent, not just in salary and commissions, but in damaged relationships, morale and lost opportunities as well.

Worksheet Estimating the Cost
of Poor Recruiting Decisions

Base Salary	$_____
Anticipated Commissions	$_____
Estimated Value of Lost Business Opportunities	$_____
Estimated Value of Damaged Relationships	$_____
Value of Training Investment Lost	$_____
Estimated Value of Negative Impact on Team Morale	$_____
Licensing Fees Lost	$_____
Estimated Value of Lost Future Sales or Renewals	$_____
Total Financial Impact for Bad Hire:	$_____

Now I want to talk for a moment about what you can, and cannot expect from this book. It is not the proverbial magic pill that will transform your business overnight, or a comprehensive pass/fail test that will automatically tell you which candidates to hire and which ones to pass by. It will not save your business from self- destruction, nor is it a gimmick that will suddenly make recruiting easy. Recruiting and coaching your team will continue to be the hardest parts of your job, because people are complex. There is just no getting around this fact.

This book will give you a system that will make recruiting the right person easier, and will begin your training on a system complete with processes, tools and skills you can use to improve your odds of hiring the right people, and therefore move your whole team forward in productivity and professionalism. It will begin the process of training in the knowledge of human behavior, a discipline that must be mastered in order to use the system properly. This system has been proven to work when used consistently.

One of our clients at Sales Manage Solutions experienced same store sales increases of 70% in one year after implementing our Best-practice Recruiting System, and at a time when their industry as a whole was experiencing flat sales. The only thing they did differently was to dramatically change their recruiting system. They used this system and trusted it to work for them.

I will caution you about expecting similar results. First, it *is* possible, but you must have, or be, a leader who is willing to put a stake in the ground and mandate that everyone is going to look for the same traits and skills in the same way, and follow the system together, to determine what works. Most companies, unfortunately, lack a leader who is willing to hold others accountable. They let individual managers monkey with the system, and water it down. It takes time to break old habits, and to come to understand that "What I am doing now really is not working." Most team leaders are reluctant to admit this, much less put forth the honest effort to take action to change, and try something new.

Just as I discovered that making great recruiting decisions is more than looking for sparkle, I hope that through this book, you will discover that learning a lot about human behavior will make you a superior recruiter and will improve your coaching skills. My hope is that you will take it to heart, and use the knowledge here to impact your sales team and every other area of your life as well. Congratulations for wanting to grow in wisdom and expertise and wanting to work hard every day for the benefit of others.

Chapter 2:

The Kind of Team You Want Dictates the Kind of Coach You Need to Become

Many sales managers correctly see themselves as coaches, and may even have served as sports coaches in their communities for children's soccer, football, baseball or basketball.

Unfortunately, that is not the kind of coach a sales leader needs to be. A community sports coach works with players who are there for extra-curricular activities, not as their primary focus. The community coach has to work within the limits of the time his or her players have available, and work with whomever shows up. Even though the caliber and skill level of players may vary greatly, there is no real training time outside of team practices for building skill sets.

If you have ever watched youngsters play "bumblebee" soccer, when the kids have not yet learned their positions or how to play as a team, and everyone runs like a swarm of bees going after the ball, then you understand what I mean—lots of enthusiasm—not much in the way of results.

Compare that to the NFL Combine, or National Invitational Camp (NIC). Anyone who wants to play in the National Football League has to go through it, and it consists of several days of grueling, precise, scientific testing—medically, psychologically and physically. The NFL describes it as "the ultimate four day job interview for the top college football players eligible for the upcoming NFL Draft." It is no wonder. There is big money on the line. Even the lowliest bench warmer in the NFL makes $300,000 or more each year. Star quarterback Peyton Manning makes $3 million a year. So those doing the hiring are making sure they get it right.

The NFL has a system that begins with a profile of the perfect NFL player, and every "wannabe" is compared against that profile. They know how tall, how smart, how strong, how proficient —everything. It is no Little League game. These guys are in it to win, to get the best in the nation, or even the world and nothing less will do. This is the kind of coach you want to be, and the type of team you want to recruit. Look at the above worksheet on the cost of poor recruiting decisions, and you will see that this analogy holds true. You have big money on the line, and you need to get it right. How do you create your own version of the NFL Combine?

My son is a golfer and at one time wanted to turn pro. In order to even try out for the circuit, he needed to raise $80,000. This is usually done through sponsorships. If he came to you and asked your company to sponsor him, how would you make your decision? You would probably start by talking to him about his game, his scoring statistics, and his aspirations. You would ask a lot of questions. Then you would likely watch him play. By the time you have done that, you have driven to the course and watched a round... you have invested at least eight hours in making this hypothetical $80,000 decision. Also, you would compare him to the best players currently on the tour, not to a few of his fellow college team players.

How many sales managers spend eight hours with a sales candidate before making a hiring decision? Yet they are going to pay the candidate fifty or a hundred thousand dollars or more annually, plus commissions. On your worksheet you have established the high cost of a poor recruiting decision. If you are average, the cost is anywhere from $50,000-$250,000 or more. I have one client that spends $500,000 per salesperson selecting and training over a twelve-month period. You need your own version of the NFL Combine. You must know the traits and skills that make up the perfect salesperson in order to build a profile to which you can compare all candidates.

How do I Know What the "Best" Looks Like?

Any sports fan who has followed a team for more than a season or two knows that the strength of a team comes from recruiting. You cannot win national championships with mediocre talent. In the pros, there is a season for hiring, but they are always in recruitment mode, watching the promising players coming out of high schools and colleges. It is an art form.

Outstanding sales managers, too, know they need to always be in recruitment mode, not just when they have an opening. Too few of them know where to look, or even what to look for. So they may not recognize diamonds when they see them.

Left to our own instincts, we like and hire people who are like us. That may make a team you like and get along with, but it is not likely to be the most effective team. With a system, you can take emotion out of the equation, and replace it with logic to evaluate your top candidates. Remember my story about the dinner party: The one who talks the most begins to like the other person. You want to be dealing with the reality of the candidate and his true profile—not your own emotions, when it comes to a hiring decision.

But we are getting ahead of ourselves. The first step is to know what you are looking for in a sales candidate, so that you recognize them when you see them, and then to know where to look for them.

> There are five key dimensions, defined in order of importance, that make up the "Best Salesperson Profile": Attitudes, Motivations, Character Traits, Personality Traits and Sales Skills.

The "Recruit the Best" system begins with the "Best Salesperson Profile". You may have heard the story popularized a number of years ago in a speech by Russell Conwell titled *Acres of Diamonds*. He tells of a man who decided to sell his family's farm and use the money from the sale to go in search of diamonds, not realizing that the rocks that riddled that family farm were, in fact, diamonds. They were uncut, diamonds in the rough, unrecognizable to the untrained eye.

You must know how to recognize diamonds when you see them. This starts with the "Best Salesperson Profile". There are five key dimensions, defined in order of importance, that make up the "Best Salesperson Profile": Attitudes, Motivations, Character Traits, Personality Traits and Sales Skills. Armed with this profile, you are in a position to start looking for candidates, and begin measuring them using this profile.

The science of hiring well has been the subject of many studies. These studies further illustrate the point of learning all you can before, like the guy in *Acres of Diamonds,* you go selling the family farm. In this case, we are trying to get enough information to make a decision which is worth a great deal of money, a decision that will impact many careers as well as your companies' future for years to come.

What do most studies show? Over 55% of the people currently in sales should not be in sales. Of the 45% who are left, about half of those can sell, but should be selling something else. That means, on average, we are making poor recruiting decisions most of the time.

It is no wonder why. Too often, we are making decisions in the dark. As mentioned earlier, traditional hiring methods yield only about 6% of the information we need to make a good decision. That comes from screening resumes (2%), conducting unstructured interviews (2%), and doing reference checks (2%). It is incredible that these three activities make up the dominant hiring system in America. With a net yield of only 6% of the information you need to make a hiring decision, it is perfectly clear why so many Americans are unhappy in their jobs. Most of them are ill-suited to the work they do, and are consequently miserable.

But if that is how most businesses recruit and hire, how does one do it differently and more reliably in terms of results?

- You use a system that is based on process, logic and measurable information instead of the typical "system" described above that yields a decision based on emotion, opinion and "I-gotta-get-some-one-in-here" urgency.

- You use the Sales Manage Solutions Best-practice Recruiting System. We have found in using this system over the past decade that it yields between 60-90% of the critical information necessary for making the right hiring decision for both you and the sales candidate. While no system is perfect and you will never have as much information as you would like to have, this greatly improves your odds of creating a winning sales team over traditional methods. We have the statistics and company growth records to prove it.

Chapter 3:

"Recruit the Best" - A Best-Practice Recruiting System

The "Recruit the Best" system has four key elements:

1) A "Best Salesperson Profile", including all five dimensions of Attitudes, Motivations, Character, Personality and Sales Skills;

2) A process to follow, including step-by-step directions from initial contact to hire;

3) Tools to use, such as structured questionnaires, assessments, and scoring or matching sheets to compare each candidate to the ideal profile;

4) Skills in interviewing, screening, and the discipline to follow the system.

I have noticed when I am reading discussion forums on LinkedIn, that sales managers often ask other sales managers, "What are some good interview questions?" This question most likely comes about because they are not hiring every week, and their interviewing skills are a little rusty. This tells me they do not have a system. Many sales managers are under the impression that a set of clever questions is the simple solution to their complex recruiting challenge. Their motivation is great; however, there are no magic or universally great questions to ask in an interview. The questions you ask must be tied to the traits and skills for which you are looking. The reality is these sales leaders on LinkedIn need all the elements of a recruiting system to solve their recruiting challenges.

At this point, we want to begin with the first element in the "Recruit the best" system - the "Best Salesperson Profile". Finding your best salespeople begins with building the "Best Salesperson Profile. This answers the question, WHAT do I look for?

When I was in high school, the school decided to form a track team for the first time in the school's history. They recruited one of the football coaches to form the team, who immediately recruited some of the football players to be on the team. To choose the team members to represent us in the long jump, he pulled three of us skinny guys over to the sand pit to see who would represent us at the next week's competition.

The first guy jumped and measured at fifteen feet. I was impressed along with the coach. The next guy jumped an astonishing eighteen feet. It was now my turn. I was feeling competitive, but not hopeful, since I had never long-jumped before. Running, jumping and using my best idea of long-jumping form, I cleared twenty feet. We were all shocked and impressed and glad to have such strong representation at our next competition.

At our first meet it was time for the long jump. I was the first to compete. Feeling confident, I got ready to show my stuff. My first competitive jump was my personal best at twenty feet, six inches. I awaited the applause. None came—no one was impressed. Confused, I moved to the sideline and watched as my competitor took a jump. His form was different, and his technique seemed more efficient as he jumped twenty-five feet. The crowd applauded. I was embarrassed but impressed. I had visions of this guy going to the Olympics, until I researched to find the world record at the time was around twenty-eight feet.

When we do not know what a best salesperson looks like, we compare each candidate against the small number of other candidates under consideration, instead of against the perfect candidate. We think twenty feet is impressive when we are unaware the world record is twenty-eight feet. Of course, we are not going to find the perfect salesperson, but unless we are comparing against perfection, we will not know the true measure of our candidate. We will not know the true strengths and weaknesses we need to measure and eventually coach.

> When we do not know what a best salesperson looks like, we compare each candidate against the small number of other candidates under consideration, instead of against the perfect candidate.

The bottom line is, wise people understand that in order to find perfection, you must know what perfection looks like. In the case of hiring sales superstars, your own version of the NFL Combine starts with knowing the profile of a sales superstar for your business or your industry. You need to define, in order: the ideal attitudes, motivations, character, personality and sales skills needed to be successful within your corporate and industry structure.

If sales candidates do not have the right attitude, the motivations and all the rest will not matter. If they do not have sufficient character, you do not want them on your team no matter how stellar their sales skills.

The "Best Salesperson Profile" answers the question, "WHAT do I look for when recruiting salespeople?"

In advance of an interview, the candidates' Facebook or LinkedIn profile gives me an opportunity to form an opinion about them prior to the meeting. However, without a specific set of guidelines

Best Salesperson Profile

1. Attitudes

2. Motivations

3. Character

4. Personality

5. Sales Skills

with which to compare them, I may be impressed by their ability to "jump twenty feet". My research becomes personal conjecture or satisfied curiosity.

Let us take each part of the "Best Salesperson Profile" and apply some definitions. Here is a brief definition of each of the five elements. In later chapters, we will further define the traits and skills and discuss the use of tools to measure how much of each trait a candidate will bring to the job.

Key Element #1: Attitude

Do the sales candidates have the type attitude that will enable them to have a passion about the product or service they will be selling? How do the candidates feel about themselves as sales-people? If they have a bad image of salespeople in general, they are not likely to have a good attitude in the long term about them-selves as salespeople. For instance, there are a lot of bad lawyer jokes that make the rounds. If you are the type person who, as a lawyer, gets offended by those jokes, you are not likely to do well in the legal field. Your sensitivity to the jokes reveals that your attitude and self-image just will not hold up. Likewise, people who do not hold salespeople in high regard will not do well in sales. If salespeople do not have a passion for solving customers' problems by using their company's product or service, sustained effort is a challenge. Honest salespeople simply cannot sell something they do not believe in.

Key Element #2: Motivations

Top salespeople always have something in their life they want to change for the better. The best-fit salesperson for your team will be motivated to benefit others by selling your product, believing this effort will help him or her achieve the desired financial goals. You want a sales candidate motivated to earn money. Candidates must have immediate financial needs, as well as long-term financial goals that will spur them on when the going gets tough. Everyone begins a new job with excitement, but sooner or later, it becomes a lot like real work. It is what I call "the Sweat Zone." Once the new salesperson hits the Sweat Zone, having sufficient motivations will see him or her through to accomplishing the desired goals. Motivation for change is very important but not sufficient. The salesperson must also possess the ability to do the job well.

Key Element #3: Character

Character is a set of four key qualities that are learned through the early influence of parents and mentors. It is about what we do when no one is looking; an internalized compass of right and wrong; a code and standard for living. You want everyone on your sales staff to represent your company well, and serve your clients with integrity. You must have salespeople with sufficient character to carry this out. The specific character qualities we are looking for are:

- Honesty
- Concern for Others
- Strong Work Ethic
- Responsibility—willingness to take responsibility for the outcomes of one's actions

Key Element #4: Personality

While character is learned, usually at a young age, personality is genetic. We are all hard-wired from birth with certain personality traits. Some of us are high-strung, others more laid-back. We could be humorous or naturally charming; extremely quick on our feet; or more thoughtful and considered when speaking. It is all part of our genetic personality. Life works much more smoothly for those who have personalities that are in alignment with the job they are doing. It is an old cliché, but very true, "Find work you love and you will never work another day in your life." Personality is what we have to thank for that ideal scenario. If our job and personality are *not* in alignment, work will drain our energy just trying to keep up.

There are eight scales of personality traits we will eventually examine, but the most important four are:

- Social Drive
- Social Confidence
- Goal-orientation
- Need for Control

To find your superstar salespeople, you must know the personality traits you need for success on your team. These are the most important four, and we will talk more about them as we get into the screening process. There are four others that have influence and are useful to know about, but are not as essential as the first four in a make-it-or-break-it way. They are:

- Detail-orientation
- Good Impression
- Need to Nurture
- Skepticism

These personality traits, or scales, have been identified, studied and measured by Dr. Larry Craft, a leader in the field of personality research who created the Craft Personality Questionnaire™ also known as the CPQ. *(Note that SHL Group Ltd. is the publisher/owner of the CPQ copyright)*. We will talk more about Dr. Craft later, and the way he and other behavioral scientists have made our job of hiring much easier by isolating the complexities of human behavior and unlocking them, providing a valuable key to being able to objectively measure personality in a practical way.

Key Element #5: Sales Skills

Attitudes, Motivations, Character and Personality tell you a great deal about whether or not a person will be capable of mastering sales skills. The question is, "How skilled in sales do you need candidates to be when they walk in the door?" Some sales leaders must rely on existing sales skills because they have neither the time nor the resources to invest in training. Others would prefer no prior sales training or skills, so there are no bad habits to un-learn. They have the time and resources for training. You must decide what you need in this area for your specific team.

If you have decided to hire people with sales skills rather than train them, you need to look for candidates who are proficient in all of the following sales skills required to sell your product:

- Prospecting/Networking
- Setting Appointments and Holding Appointments
- Fact-finding/Discovering Needs
- Presenting Solutions
- Handling Objections, Fears and Concerns
- Closing Sales

One More Key Element – Learning Style

Even though I have not included learning style as one of the five key elements in the "Best Salesperson Profile", it is never the less, an important factor. The learning style piece of the puzzle can be confusing. We all know people who can easily obtain a degree, but they struggle to earn a living due to other missing key elements. We also know many salespeople who do not have a college degree, but have a very successful career. When it comes to selecting salespeople, we want to make sure that they have the capacity to quickly gain the necessary knowledge needed to do their job well, and also that they have the discipline to continue to increase their industry knowledge and sales expertise.

It is important for salespeople to have the capacity to quickly learn the following types of information:

- Information to obtain the necessary licenses
- Features and benefits of the product/service they will be selling
- Features and benefits of all major competitors products
- Market demographics
- Customer demographics
- Sales and marketing strategies
- Face-to-face sales processes

To measure learning styles, I recommend looking at grades and learning style tests. The "Oxford Learning Aptitude Survey", which is available through www.CraftProfiles.com is one way to measure intelligence. Also, the "Wonderlic Cognitive Ability Test" is another popular assessment.

Learning style is easier to discern when the candidates have high grades, score high on learning style tests and have a track record of success in the same or related industries for which you are recruiting. It is more difficult when candidates score high on Attitudes, Motivations, Character Traits and Personality Traits, but score low on learning style tests, have little to no education beyond high school, and have no experience selling in your industry.

I trust the above mentioned learning style tests only at the moderate to high scores. I have found that people who score in the higher ranges of these tests are quick learners and will most likely not struggle with learning the things needed to sell your product. However, I have also seen candidates who score in the lower ranges on these tests be perfectly capable of learning the things necessary to be great salespeople. Many quick learners, for a variety of reasons, are not good test takers. Things in their past have programmed them to react negatively while taking tests.

If a candidate has a low score on a learning style test, I ask these questions:

- What were your grades in high school and/or college?
- How long did it take you to finish your college degree?
- While you were getting your education, what other activities were you involved in?
- What books have you read in the past twelve months?
- What magazines, trade journals and blogs do you read?
- What seminars and training programs have you attended in the past?
- What are some subjects that sufficiently arouse your curiosity that cause you to research and learn about those particular subjects? Tell me some things you have learned.

If the candidates are working hard to gain knowledge that help advance their careers and have a well rounded interest in other subjects, it is very likely that they will work hard to learn the things they need to know to sell your product. I have also found that these salespeople may be more willing to operate beyond their natural personality tendencies. For example, knowledgeable salespeople with low scores on the Social Confidence trait will find it easier to push themselves outside their comfort zone more readily than the person who scores low on the Social Confidant trait and struggles with learning complex information.

Chapter 4:

You Have Built a "Best Salesperson Profile" — Now What?

The First Tool in the "Recruit the Best" System – "Matching Score Sheet"

Now that we have defined our "Best Salesperson Profile", we need to be able to measure, objectively, how each of our sales candidates stacks up against this ideal. To do that, we have created a tool called the Matching Score Sheet. I encourage you to use it every time you have a hiring decision to make.

Remember, every good system involves a process, tools and skills. The Matching Score Sheet is the first tool in the system. It is essential to your success. This tool helps you score all five dimensions (Attitudes, Motivations, Character, Personality and Sales Skills) on a scale of one to ten.

I hope you realize by now that the attitude "I know enough about selling that I can teach anybody to sell" just does not hold true. There are too many factors involved, and too much at stake to trust that kind of bravado or naïveté. You want to be as scientific about recruiting and hiring as you can be to insure the best possible chance for success. You need a system that enables you to search and compare candidates to see how they measure up against your ideal salesperson profile. Then you will be able to choose your first round draft pick.

Score a person in the Five Key Areas listed above. Use the Tool (on page 186-187) called Best Salesperson Matching Score Sheet, and start using it the moment you start to like a candidate. It never fails to amaze me how well this process works, or how easily we can fool ourselves if we fail to use the systems available to us.

> Compare an emotional decision to the "Recruit the Best" system, which is very logical and standard-ized. The system gives you a process to follow and tools for collecting far more concrete information on which to base your decision.

My business partner, Lance Cooper, is the best sales coach I know. We had worked with a company for a number of years, and the owners knew the system, had built their ideal candidate profile, educated their managers on how to use it, and trained them as to its importance. They had done everything "right." There were about three candidates that were vying for the job position that was open. As Lance was coaching the hiring manager, the manager preferred one candidate over all the others. "How does he score?" Lance asked.

The manager had not yet even filled out the Best Salesperson Matching Score Sheet on the candidates. He thought he knew and understood the system well enough to do it in his head, using his "experience" or his "gut." He had not really done the true work necessary to hire the best. The manager instinctively liked the candidate he thought would be the top scorer. But, when they sat down and ran the numbers against the ideal profile, it was another candidate who won the day.

I need to say this again: *do not just trust your gut*. Do not let yourself make an emotional hiring decision that is wrong. In other words, do not get "snowed". Develop the discipline to use a system to improve your odds in hiring the best salesmen out there, and improve your sales team and profits by doing so.

The general dynamic of the selection process is this:

> Candidates apply to work for us, and they come prepared to put their best foot forward, creating a profile for us to see during the selection process. Their profile includes their resume, answers to interview questions, references and so forth.

> Our job as sales team leaders in search of our next superstar is to unwrap the package and evaluate the candidate's profile to determine if he or she has the traits and skills needed to survive and succeed in a high-activity, high-rejection environment. We must measure the degree to which this candidate is growing or declining in all areas of his or her profile.

In fact, we must measure the candidates against our prepared "Best Salesperson Profile" to see how they compare to our "ideal" candidate. We do this knowing that there are no "perfect" candidates. By going through the process of comparison, we can see which of the candidates in the running for a particular job opening is the *best* fit. We know the areas in which the candidates will need attention and coaching, should we choose to hire them.

Steps to "Recruit the Best" System

The reason typical hiring methods yield such poor decision-making information is that there is no measurement or standardization involved in evaluating or collecting the information. Hence, you not only get about 6% of what you need from the entire process, but you greatly increase your chances of getting it wrong, because you are simply making an emotional decision.

Compare an emotional decision to the "Recruit the Best" system, which is very logical and standardized. The system gives you a process to follow and tools for collecting far more concrete information on which to base your decision.

The "Recruit the Best" system contains three stages. After finding great candidates using a network of referral sources, we move the candidates through these three stages: Screening, Profiling and Interviewing.

Stage 1 - "Screening"

In this stage, we screen resumes, then screen by phone using our "Phone Screen Questionnaire". Next, we send the stronger candidates an "Email Questionnaire" for further screening. Those candidates who make it past these steps are sent a "Homework Assignment" in preparation for the initial face-to-face interview. This assignment is a simple task. The candidate is directed to click on the link provided in the email to view information about the company and career.

We conduct this first in-person interview using the "Initial Interview Questionnaire". Candidates who pass this stage, are asked to provide six references as described later. (This stage provides 20-30% of the information needed to hire well.)

The tools and questionnaires described here are available online at www.CanTheySell.com. Please visit the site and purchase downloadable copies.

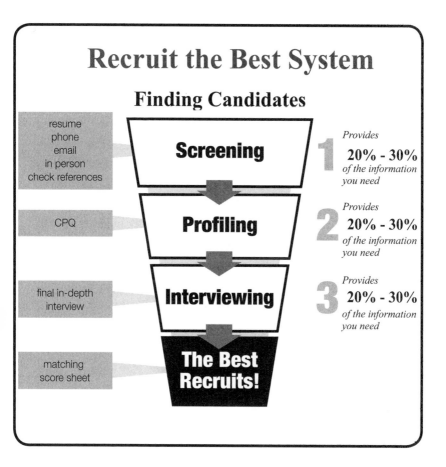

Stage 2 - "Profiling"

In this stage, we take the stronger candidates and administer a personality assessment to test for personality traits in line with our "Best Salesperson Profile". For the past eleven years I have used the Craft Personality Profile (CPQ), which we will talk more about later. (This stage provides 20-30% of the information needed to hire well.)

Stage 3 - "Interviewing"

In this stage, we conduct an in-depth interview using the "In-depth Interview Questionnaire." This is a final "Cross Check" interview. You should know the applicant pretty well by now. This final interview is your opportunity to address any lingering issues, and to re-confirm what you may have discovered or concluded in previous steps. At the end of this stage, you should have a really good measure of the candidate's strengths and weaknesses. (This step provides a final 20-30% of the information needed to hire well.)

You are now ready to fill out the "Matching Score Sheet". Here you will give the candidate a score in each of the five areas of the "Best Salesperson Profile".

Note: Some choose to give the CPQ prior to the first face-to-face interview. There are two schools of thought. Some are in a situation where their time to conduct the initial interview is more valuable than the cost of the CPQ. Others have more time to invest in the initial interview, so they wait to order the CPQ if the candidate passes the interview. It is all a matter of the cost of your time. I have seen both approaches work equally well.

The Second Tool in the "Recruit the Best" System— "Recruit the Best Checklist"

On page 188, you will find a checklist of the steps to follow for each candidate. This list will guide you through all three stages of the "Recruit the Best" system. Use this checklist with every candidate. After you complete a step, check it as completed. This tool will help you stay focused and disciplined during the recruiting process. Keep a copy of this sheet in the file of all candidates to aid in your discussion with other members of your recruiting team.

Remember not to skip a step. The temptation is to rush those candidates who you like through the process. This checklist, along with the "Matching Score Sheet", helps you make a logical rather than an emotional recruiting decision.

Chapter 5:

Developing Your Interviewing Skills

Have you ever listened in frustration to news conferences with polished politicians? Reporters ask questions, but the politicians never really answer in a direct or concrete way. Job interviews can be the same way if you let them.

I once asked a sales leader candidate to tell me about a situation, real or imagined, where a sales rep was at 30% of quota at the middle of the month. What would he do or say to coach the sales rep to get him to reach quota by the end of the month?

Instead of giving me a specific example that answered my question, the sales leader candidate attempted to skirt around the question with his polished philosophy of the importance of sales targets. I finally had to interrupt him and say, "Have you had a conversation in the past several weeks with one of your sales reps using the philosophy of sales targets that you just described to me." He said, "Yes". I had to tell him, "Please tell me that story of what you did with the sales rep and what was the outcome." He again gave me a very vague general story. After this second failed attempt, it was easy for me to see that he did not really understand sales metrics or how to use metrics to coach his sales reps. In the end, it was clear that while he talked a good game, he did not have the experience we were looking for. Not long thereafter, I had an almost identical answer on the same question. When I told the candidate to tell me a story of when she used her philosophy with an actual sales rep, she gave me a great story of how she actually helped the rep succeed. It was clear that she knew how to apply her knowledge. It is important to have the right questions and to get at the real answer to be able to measure specific attributes.

As an interviewer, it is important in the interview that you get *specific* examples of when the candidate has done *specific* things to get a *specific* result. What you are looking for is a *specific* plan. i.e. the way the candidates track their activities, and hold themselves accountable to the goal. Many interviewees can give you philosophy and eloquence and, if you are not listening very carefully, or you are having a low energy day, you might be influenced by their eloquence.

Learning to conduct an effective face-to-face interview is a skill that must be developed. When you handle yourself in a very professional manner in which you put the burden on the candidate to sell you, your job becomes easier. Strong candidates naturally shine without your effort to befriend them. Weaker candidates naturally struggle when you act professionally without a "we-really-need-you-here" attitude.

> I have two interviewing secrets that will quickly make anyone a master interviewer.

I remember working with a new client on a project to hire a sales leader. Part of the project was for the client and me to interview candidates together. After the interviews, the President of the division told me, "The candidates said you were a nice and professional guy, but a brutal interviewer. They said they had never been through anything like that. What did you *do?*" The answer to what they thought was "so brutal" was simple. I explained to the President, "I read the questions and did not talk."

I have two interviewing secrets that will quickly make anyone a master interviewer. One, I am always armed with specific questions tied to my "Best Salesperson Profile". Two, I simply read the questions, record the information and move to the next question. I know what I am looking for, and I have the tools to look for it. I always remain calm and confident during the interview. I keep very neutral facial expressions being careful to not nod my head in agreement. I avoid adding my own stories, which can inadvertently lead the candidate. The real secret to getting the truth from an interviewee is in the silence. Just read the question and be quiet. If they do not answer the question, I ask it again. After the second attempt, I assume they do not have a good answer.

X Factor creator and judge Simon Cowell is very good at this. You know what he is thinking afterwards because he will tell you, but he offers no encouragement, feedback or direction while contestants are performing. They have to generate it themselves. L.A. Reid, on the other hand, is leading the contestant during the entire performance by nodding his head with the beat. By his body language, he is encouraging and directing the contestant the entire time. At that point, the contestant is focused on encouraging or changing L.A.'s reaction, not on genuinely being himself or herself.

Simon is the better judge because he makes the contestants give their true performance without encouragement or tips from him. They must generate it all from within. They must bring their top performance to the evaluation stage. He is a master at understanding the personal uniqueness of contestants.

Most of your interviewees are good performers. If you give them any clues, or interact with them, they will put on their game

> You may be thinking that you risk offending great candidates and not making them feel welcome. It is quite the opposite. Great candidates like the challenge this type of interview presents. Confident salespeople rise to the challenge and do their best whether the interviewer is warm and engaging or unemotional. Strong candidates are more attracted to the pleasantly calm and confident manager than to the "sell-them-on-the-career" type manager.

face and "go to town" performing. Give them no clues, and you get their genuine uniqueness. Sometimes it is pretty; other times it is ugly; but you know the truth.

When candidates leave the interview and, when asked how the interview went, their answer should be, "I am not sure. I really got no reaction from the interviewer as to how I was doing." This reaction is an indication of a successful interview. You get the raw, non-embellished information you need to make a hiring decision when you keep your emotions hidden during the interview.

You may be thinking that you risk offending great candidates and not making them feel welcome. It is quite the opposite. Great candidates like the challenge this type of interview presents. Confident salespeople rise to the challenge and do their best whether the interviewer is warm and engaging or unemotional. Strong candidates are more attracted to the pleasantly calm and confident manager than to the "sell-them-on-the-career" type manager.

My wife has always known about the power of keeping your

emotions in check during difficult conversations. Maybe because she does not like to talk much, she is a better listener. Whatever the reason, she has always known how to direct the conversation through silence. When my children were either being punished or struggling with something, she would let them talk, and then she would ask a question. She let them talk some more. By the end of the conversation, they had talked themselves into the very thing she wanted them to do.

If a parent sits in front of a child and shows love to that child, it turns on the "I want to do the right thing" button, and disengages the rebellion button. From my wife, I learned that all you have to do to touch that "I want to do the right thing" button is show them love; you do that by giving them your full attention. You listen.

When we have a great set of interview questions and show the candidates respect by listening carefully to their answers, they will tell us all we need to know for us to measure their traits and skills. Many times they even reveal helpful personal information about themselves that we legally cannot ask.

Do Your Homework

I always recommend assigning "homework" to the candidates, to see how aggressively they will work to get the job. It is a good idea to do some of our own homework on the candidates before they arrive. Our celebrity-obsessed culture makes it OK to post every detail of our lives on Facebook and elsewhere—it gives us what pop culture icon Andy Warhol dubbed our "15 minutes of fame." So take advantage of all this in-depth information candidates post on the Internet. Before you interview candidates, read their Facebook posts and Linkedin profile. You will learn a lot about them from the things they share about their lives.

The following are some additional tips for interviewing:

- Listen at least eighty percent of the time; do not talk more than twenty percent of your time together.

- Do not grill the candidate. Merely ask the questions, and move on.

- Ask for specific examples. Do not settle for vague, general answers to questions.

- Ask the questions exactly as they are written. Do not preface the question with information (this leads the candidate). Do not restate the question. If the candidate does not understand or wants clarification, tell him to answer the question based on his best understanding of the question.

- Ask all the questions in order. Do not skip around.

- Follow the system as written.

- It is OK to interrupt the candidate. If a candidate rambles, ask "What was my question?" Smart candidates will get the hint about rambling.

- Until the end of the process, do not sell the candidate on the career. Sell her on the process as a mutual fit discovery for both parties. The strongest candidate will sell you on her abilities.

- After the candidate answers the question, move to the next question. Do not react emotionally. Do not tell a personal story that relates to the example the candidate just gave you. Do not tell the candidate that you understand how he/she feels. Do not say, "I would have done the same thing." Do not answer the question, "What would you have done?"

Tips for Keeping It Legal

One side note here regarding the interview process. **Never promise to call candidates back,** or let them know how they did. Say instead, "Thank you for answering my questions today. We are looking at a lot of candidates. As I continue to evaluate candidates, I will keep your information in mind." There are several reasons for telling the candidate this. There are some candidates I am not at all interested in, and I do not want to lead them on. If I am interested, I ask the candidates, "What questions do you have for me?" This gives the candidates the perfect opportunity to ask me about the next step. Strong candidates are always asking, "What's next?" "Do I get the job?"

It is also a good idea not to tell them they flunked, even if they did. It can get you into legal, social or emotional trouble, so it is best not to give evaluations of their interview. Just a "Thank you for your time" is fine. Repeat, "We are looking at many candidates, and I will keep your information in mind." Leave it at that. It is your job to pick a candidate, not give career advice. Even with the best intentions, you expose yourself to multiple lawsuits if you start talking too much or are too candidly with the candidate.

Tell the candidates that you are looking for the best of the best, a top performer to be on the team, someone who can rise to the top in a fast-paced, high-activity high-rejection environment. Let them sell you on why he or she is the right person for the job. Let them know that this is a great place to work on a strong team for the right person. Do not paint an unrealistic picture by telling them, for example, that this is a fun place to work with low stress. Do use the Matching Sheet. Do not get emotionally excited about a candidate and skip steps in the process.

Sample Questions from the "Recruit the Best Initial Interview Questionnaire"

Measuring Personality Traits

Goal-orientation

1. How do you rank yourself in your Drive to Set and Reach Goals? 1 - 2 - 3 - 4 - 5 - 6 - 7 - 8 - 9 - 10

2. What are some best examples of how you have used your natural abilities in Setting and Reaching Goals? *(Strong candidates will have several specific examples of goals/outcomes achieved. Weaker candidates will have difficulty being specific about goals/outcomes, or may admit they are not as driven as they should be.)*

3. What are some areas in your life where your lack of goal drive has kept you from achieving at your best? *(The strong candidate will have a hard time coming up with a good answer to this question. The weaker candidate will make excuses and blame others for not reaching goals.)*

Social Confidence

1. How do you rank yourself in your confidence when you are dealing with people? 1 - 2 - 3 - 4 - 5 - 6 - 7 - 8 - 9 - 10

2. What are some examples of how your Social Confidence has helped you in dealing with people, and in getting something that you wanted and felt was important. *(Strong candidates will give several specific examples of situations where they have exerted their confidence in dealing with people. Weaker candidates will talk more about confidence in doing a task.)*

3. What are some examples of when your lack of Social Confidence has hindered you in dealing with people? *(Strong candidates will have a hard time coming up with specific examples. Weaker candidates will make excuses and blame others or admit they are not as confident as they should be.)*

Social Drive

Put yourself in this picture. We go to a chamber of commerce networking event where 100 people have gathered to network with each other. You see one of your best friends across the room. You do not know anyone else in the room. Your mission is to spend the next two hours in the room getting to know as many people as possible. At the end of the two hours, you and I meet to discuss your success. *(It is important that you simply read this paragraph. Additional details are not necessary. The candidate's facial expressions will tell you a lot about their Social Drive. Do they wince at the thought of having to do this task, or do they get excited about it?)*

1. How many people are going to remember meeting you?

2. How did you go about meeting the most people?

3. What are some examples in your life where you have been put into a new situation where you had to develop a lot of new relationships?

4. After a week in this new situation, what percent of the new people knew who you were?

5. How do you feel about public speaking? What is your experience in public speaking?

Need for Control

1. Think of a time in school or at a retreat when you were put into a group. Describe your desires to get the group organized and moving forward. *(High need for control candidates will describe themselves as eager to take charge and get things moving ahead. Low need for control people will speak of letting someone else take control and lead.)*

2. Long-term, in your career, do you prefer to continue to work under a supervisor or work independently?

For the complete questionnaire, visit www.CanTheySell.com.

Getting to The Truth

If you just cannot get to the truth about a candidate because they continue to exaggerate their strengths and downplay their weaknesses, the following interview technique may work. It is the best interview technique I have learned, for which I must give credit to *Who: The A Method for Hiring* by Geoff Smart and Randy Street.

Ask these questions:

- Who did you report to at XYZ Company? How do you spell that?

- When I call him and ask him about your strengths, what will he tell me?

- When I ask him about your greatest weaknesses, what will he tell me?

- When I ask him about how well you manage your time (or any other area you are concerned about), what will he likely to tell me?

Techniques for Dealing with References

My philosophy in asking for references is totally different from the typical process of randomly calling former bosses, or people the candidates may have mentioned or who might know them. It is also challenging to call the references that they have put on their resumes, because of the problem we have in our society of people having their hands tied by our legal system, and not being able to speak candidly about a candidate.

I tell them, "I want you to provide me with six references, the names and telephone numbers of six people who will talk to me and will say good things about you when I call them. I want two former bosses, two former co-workers, and two former customers."

If they do not yet have any sales experience, I ask for two business owners or successful business people they know in the community that can vouch for their character. Many people fail this assignment by not providing the two references in the three categories as requested.

When asking for a co-worker, make it clear that you do not want someone who has worked for the candidates, or someone for whom they have worked; you want a peer, someone who is familiar with the challenges they have faced, and how they work and handle themselves.

> Asking for these references is somewhat equivalent to the recommendations someone might post on their LinkedIn profile. Strong salespeople quickly come up with the requested six references in each category.

Asking for these references is somewhat equivalent to the recommendations someone might post on their LinkedIn profile. Strong salespeople quickly come up with the requested six references in each category. Weak and moderate salespeople struggle with this exercise. I have gotten names with phone numbers that do not work. Seriously, how hard would it have been for them to call ahead, straighten out the logistical details and give their references a heads up? I have to conclude that if they are not willing to put forth great effort on this exercise, they most likely will not put forth great effort to take care of my customers.

Strong salespeople call their references in advance and tell them I'll be calling, and tell them to say good things when I call. Many times I have been on the fence with a candidate and this one exercise helped me make an easy decision. Sometimes you get really lucky, and they give you the name of a reference that you know. That is great for you in getting information about a candidate, but not always so great for the candidate.

Once I was working with a client company to hire a new sales rep. We thought we might hire her. I was hopeful and so was the company management. Then, one of the references she provided was someone I knew really well. I thought, jackpot! I am about to get confirmation that we are making a great hire. I called our mutual friend, and the first words out of her mouth were, "Oh, you are interviewing crazy Kathy!"

Another time, I was interviewing a sales manager candidate, and two of the six people whose phone numbers HE had provided did not work. He did not get the job. I had to assume he must not have wanted it badly enough.

Many managers who take this advice relay stories to me about the great information they get about candidates from references, dispelling their initial doubts about this step in the process. Most of the time the referral source says good things about the candidate, and many times will give additional information about some of the challenges the candidate has. These may not be challenges that are significant enough that you would not select the candidate for the job, but the information from the referral source is information that you will need for coaching and training.

When I train sales leaders and management, and we talk about their hiring techniques, I always ask them to raise their hands if they check references, and find that almost no one does. When I ask why, they tell me it is because of labor laws - no one will talk to them. So rather than battling people who will not talk to you, put the weight on the candidate to find people you can talk to. It can be well worth the effort in giving you information you need to avoid a bad hire, or make a great one.

When you do talk to the references (and be sure that you do) only take 5-8 minutes to ask the reference questions. Do not grill the reference source. Use this time to ask the reference source additional questions regarding concerns you may have discovered during the process. Ask the additional questions in an "Oh-by-the-way" fashion. "Oh by the way, is Richard well organized? How does he do at multi-tasking". "Oh by the way, how does Cathy do in managing her time? How driven would you say she is?"

Complete reference check questionnaires can be found at www.CanTheySell.com.

Building Your Recruiting Team:

Do you do it all yourself? Do you delegate to others? If so, who in your organization should be involved in recruiting and at what level should they be involved?

Companies who regularly recruit and hire in large numbers need a recruiting team. Building this team is critical. Many organizations give great attention to this important detail while others naively delegate the recruiting function to inexperienced staff. If you accept the fact that each recruiting decision puts $100,000 + at risk, it is wise to have the most competent people doing the most important steps in the process.

Let us begin with an important but simple analogy. Professional sports teams hire former successful athletes as talent scouts because their experience as an athlete gives them an important perspective on what it takes to compete at a high level. The scout has lived the life of a competitive athlete. The personal experience of competing for a place on the team, coming from behind and winning the game, sweating it out in practice to earn a first string position and playing at a professional level gives the scout an innate knowledge of what to look for and how to look for it when searching for the best of the best players.

Members of your recruiting team who have never been in sales, or have never succeeded in sales, simply have not acquired these innate skills to competently search for and select great salespeople. They may get lucky occasionally, but to get it right on a regular basis is simply an unrealistic expectation. Therefore, it is critical to have highly competent people performing the important steps. It is a mistake to rely on the human resources department to source and select sales candidates. Human Resources plays an important function, but it is not their responsibility to build a recruiting referral network of trusted referral sources and make the critical decision of whether or not a person can sell.

I see companies, dozens in fact, who delegate the sourcing, screening and initial selecting to young, inexperienced, non-sales oriented, professional looking young people who have never experienced the sweat zone of the sales profession. If you have never played the game at a competitive level, it is impossible to instill into others the skills and knowledge necessary to recognize top salespeople, much less attract the type of person you are seeking.

Please excuse my frankness here. I get a lot of pushback from sales managers who think recruiting is easy and should be handled by someone at a lower pay grade. Recruiting results is the responsibility of the manager. The important tasks of selection and attraction cannot be delegated to people with little to no sales and recruiting experience. Accept this fact as the reality of building a strong sales team and your recruiting results will take a quick turn for the better.

As you are assembling your team, consider this structure. Clerical tasks of posting jobs, and collecting resumes can be delegated. Deciding where to place the job posting and building a referral network takes skill and sales experience. People refer strong candidates to you because of your mutual relationship. It is difficult to expect your contacts to immediately develop a trusting relationship with a young, charismatic recruiter they just met.

Now that you have the "Best Salesperson Profile", and you have defined job requirements, you can delegate the initial screening of resumes to someone who understands what it takes to be in sales. It is possible to train someone experienced in sales to conduct the initial phone screen. Screening out the people who look good on paper, but sound bad on the phone, and who cannot communicate in writing on the email screen, is a task to delegate.

Those candidates who make it past the resume screen, phone screen and email screen will then be interviewed. The person conducting the initial interview must be experienced in sales at a high level, experienced in interviewing salespeople and have knowledge of human behavior. If you do not have the resources to hire this experienced person, do it yourself. That is, of course, if you are trained and use a best-practice recruiting system.

Understanding why you are asking an interview question, interpreting the information in order to score the candidate on predefined traits and skills, and seeing through the charm and charisma of mediocre salespeople requires wisdom and discernment obtained from having succeeded at the job for which you are recruiting. Realize it is your responsibility, and become a master recruiter.

If you hire a recruiting firm, make sure they are employing people similar to the sport scout mentioned above. If you are reading this book, you most likely are not looking for advice on selecting a recruiting firm.

Chapter 6:

Finding the Best Talent

So you have an idea of what you are looking for, you have brushed up on your interviewing skills and you have an idea of how to compare and contrast the various candidates. Where do you find them in the first place?

It is a great question, and the answers are nearly as numerous as there are people. The number one job of a sales manager is recruiting. The better you recruit, the easier your job is. You need to always be recruiting,

> **The number one key to recruiting is in knowing where to look.**

not just when you have an opening. Still, it is harder for some than others. If you have a small sales team with low turnover, your recruiting skills may get a little rusty between hires. Other sales managers are hiring every week or at least every month, so they have the opportunity to hone their skills a bit more and keep them sharp.

Whether you recruit every month or once a year, your number one job is recruiting. You need to get good at it, and stay good at it.

The number one key to recruiting is in knowing where to look. Sales leaders recruiting in their own communities have an advantage over those recruiting nationally. Local people have networks in their proverbial backyards. Those recruiting nationally have to reach a little further, but have essentially the same processes. Nationwide recruiters may not have the luxury of community relationships, although social networking is making the task a little easier.

The point is, whether national or local, establish a personal recruiting network. Just as a salesperson digs and builds a network of people who can make referrals for product and service sales, sales leaders need a network of people who can refer strong candidates. Remember, you are not only looking for people to interview, you are also looking for people who know people you would want to interview. Good social media and community connections can help this happen faster, without having to go through traditional mass media channels.

A company once hired me to find and hire a Sales Manager.

> Creating a network of people who are continuously sending you top recruits will give you a constant flow of great resumes, not just when you need to hire a salesperson.

I asked every other Sales Manager in the company to post on their collective social networks before they spent a dime on traditional job posting ads, and of course I posted to my networks as well. It paid off quickly. We found three good candidates in half the time allotted for the search, all from social networking. Remember, your best source for new employees is current employees and their associates. They know what it takes to do this job, and they are not going to send you someone who cannot perform.

Unfortunately, most sales managers focus on getting people who do not have jobs to come into the office for an interview, rather than on creating a network of people who will constantly send them a steady stream of qualified candidates, regardless of their current employment status. One manager I worked with told me that he was tired of looking for pearls among the cow patties. He said he was ready to "Start panning for gold using 21st century hydraulic equipment." He wanted a recruiting system like the NFL Combine we talked about earlier.

Creating a network of people who are continuously sending you top recruits will give you a constant flow of great resumes, not just when you need to hire a salesperson. If you have been in sales management for any length of time, you know that you always need a funnel of fresh prospective candidates. You never know when you will need to fill a position on the team. Do not wait until you have an opening to recruit.

It is dangerous when you have an opening to have a too-small pool of candidates from which to choose. You might feel desperate, because when there is no salesperson, there are no sales in a territory. You want to fill the slot as soon as possible. When the pool of candidates is too small, we have a tendency to pick the "best of the litter" rather than measuring all candidates against the ideal candidate we need to hire. When it comes to successful sales management, as we have discovered, it is all about recruiting. When it comes to successful recruiting, it is all about who you know—that is, those you know who know lots of others.

For the most part, the candidates who are referred to you will not be at a higher skill level than the people who refer them. Build your referral relationships mostly with people who are at the same success level as the salespeople you wish to recruit.

In recruiting, timing is everything. Finding great candidates at the time they are looking for a life change is key, which is where consistent recruiting through many sources pays off. Ideally, you should schedule time each week to meet with a referral source. Remember that no one cares as much about your business as you do, so with frequent contact, you will avoid the "out-of-sight, out-of-mind" challenge.

The great guerilla marketer, Jay Levinson, once told us in a seminar, "I am giving you 100 ways to guerilla market your product. Use as many of the 100 sources as possible." Utilize all sources. You never know from which source a candidate will come, so you must use as many sources as you can. This approach to recruiting is very proactive and intentional. Once you have these referral sources built, this list will become one of your most valuable assets.

Knowing those who know your next sales superstars may be more of a challenge if you are recruiting from (or for) out of town positions. You may need to travel to the market for which you are searching, in order to begin building your network. Still, all the above methods and ideas will work. They will just take a bit more time to develop since they are not pre-existing relationships that are virtually in your own backyard.

Following is a list of sources to consider putting into your network of referral sources. Whether you are recruiting nationally or locally, these sources are listed in order of the quality of referrals they will produce.

Best Sources:

- **Current Customers** – This is one of your strongest sources. One, it is a long list. Two, they know you, like you, and respect your company.

- **Your Database of Contacts other than Customers** – This is the list of contacts you keep in your address book. Send an email to all of them on a regular basis.

- **Current Sales Reps** – They understand what it takes to do well at your company. The people they refer are usually strong candidates. Get them to regularly email their database of non-customer contacts.

- **Sales Trainers and Sales Consultants** – Sales training franchise owners like Sandler Sales and Dale Carnegie always have a stack of resumes. Conduct a Google search for these in all the cities in which you recruit.

- **Networking Groups** – All cities have groups who meet on a regular basis to exchange referrals. These groups are full of the type of people whom you want to recruit. These include Business Networking International (BNI), eWomen Network, and many others which can be found by searching Google under "networking groups". Contact the directors/presidents of these groups. They are the most networked people in every community. They always have a stack of resumes and are usually willing to email blast your job posting to their thousands of members.

- **LinkedIn** – If you are not yet very active on LinkedIn, it is time to enter the 21st century. Social networking sites are where strong candidates look for jobs and post valuable information you will need while evaluating them. A recent post I made on Linkedin received 120 hits in three days. I not only post the job on my "Status", but also on all the groups of which I am a member. Many resources on how to best use Linkedin can be found on Google.

- **Facebook** – Regularly post to your wall an announcement that you are recruiting for your team. Tell everyone that you are growing your team so you do not leave the impression that you have high turnover. Create a Facebook fan page for recruiting. Mari Smith is a guru of Facebook fan pages. Look her up at marismith.com and follow her formula. Post the job opening on all Facebook fan pages you have "liked."

- **Other social networking platforms** - This is an ever-changing landscape. At the writing of this book, Google+ is becoming a strong social networking platform. Twitter should also be used. Post tweets on a regular basis.

Moderate Sources:

- **Churches, synagogues, temples, etc.** – With 10% unemployment, every large religious organization has a jobs ministry. Call and ask to speak to the person in charge of this ministry. Get your position posted in all of their communication sources.

- **Small Business Accountants** – Professionals who work with small businesses know those who, due to the economy, need to go back to work for someone else. Many small business owners are looking to leave the entrepreneurial track and get back into sales. They are usually great salespeople.

- **Small Business Attorneys** – Just like accountants, they know the business owner who is looking for a change.

- **Chamber of Commerce Salespeople** – They usually know all the great salespeople in town, and know people who are looking for sales positions. Attend all Chamber networking events. They are full of salespeople.

- **Presidents of Community Service Organizations** – Rotary Club, Lions Club, etc. These community leaders are all very well connected. Some may be mentoring young sales superstars.

- **Post at Salesblogcast.com** – This blog has a job board. Find other blogs with similar job postings.

- **Job Fairs** – If you recruit in large numbers, this is a way to get many people interested in your position. Attend the job fairs in your city, or hold your own. Go to jobfairtips.com for a number of useful tips. A word of warning—you will get many unqualified people coming to your job fair along with many strong candidates.

Weaker Sources:

Many sales leaders are shocked that the following sources appear in the "weaker" category since these are their most frequently used sources. Many of the candidates you find in these sources are your weaker candidates. To find the best salespeople who are looking for a change, you must use all of the above sources along with these sources.

- **Job Boards like Monster, Career Builder, etc.** – Be prepared to spend hours sifting through hundreds of resumes to find a few qualified candidates.

- **Newspapers** – This source is quickly becoming a thing of the past. Many top salespeople do not look at this source due to the high number of low paying, high turnover, lower-end sales positions that use this source.

- **Craig's List** – You will wade through many resumes; however, I found one of my best employees here.

- **College Career Services Department** – If you are not looking for people with sales experience, most universities have career placement departments and will work diligently to help you find the right candidates.

- **Industry Publications** – Most industries have magazines, journals, and online resources with job boards.

Here is a sample email, and a sample job-posting ad. The words you use in ads and while explaining the position to your referral sources are important. Using the words below will help give a clear description of the profile of a top salesperson. The wording has been chosen to attract the right candidate and to repel the wrong candidate.

Sample email to send to your current customers or list of contacts:

"Please assist me in helping someone you know. I have an open position on my sales team. If you know the right candidates for this job, please help them find a great career by sending them to see me. The right candidates will have the following traits: Honesty, hard Work Ethic, a Concern for Others and personal Responsibility. Strong candidates will have personalities which cause them to love to network to find prospects, are goal driven, and highly confident. Sales experience* ... Please have them forward their resume to me at ... Thank you for helping me find the right individuals and for helping them to find a great career."

Sales experience - fill in your desired level of sales experience based on your training resources.

Sample Wording for Job Posting:

"Salespeople wanted. ABC Company is looking for salespeople to work in the city of Nashville calling on customers to sell widgets. Requirements: Must have the following traits: Honesty, hard Work Ethic, a Concern for Others and personal Responsibility. Strong candidates will have a personality which causes them to love to network to find prospects, are goal driven, and highly confident. Sales experience ... Please forward resume to..."

Add additional information and requirements about the position as necessary. You may also consider putting a more detailed job description on your Website and add the URL to the posting. Putting a URL in the posting puts an additional challenge for the candidate to spend time reviewing the information. Strong candidates spend the time to read and study the posting and are prepared with knowledge of the position and questions.

Part II:

The Past Predicts the Future

Attitudes, Motivation and Character Traits Predict Mastery of Sales Skills

So far we have answered the question, "WHERE do I find enough candidates to interview?" The answer: You build a "Recruiting Referral Network". We have answered the question, "WHAT do I look for when assessing candidates?" The answer: You look for the five elements in the "Best Salesperson Profile". We have answered the question, "HOW do I look for the traits and skills of top salespeople?" The Answer: You learn the skills, use the tools, and follow the processes in the "Recruit the Best" system. The rest of this book will expand further on the explanation of the traits and skills found in the "Best Salesperson Profile" – Attitudes, Motivations, Character Traits, Personality Traits and Sales Skills - and teach you how to ask questions and use the Craft Personality Questionnaire (CPQ) to further score candidates on each of the five dimensions.

On the next page is a graph showing the impact the first four dimensions have on sales skills.

The more candidates possess of the first four dimensions, the more energized they become when working in sales. The fewer of the four dimensions they possess, the more their energy is drained when performing sales tasks. When we constantly perform tasks that quickly drain our energy, we naturally gravitate toward occupations where we more easily master the skills necessary to perform at a high level. This fact is the reason the first four dimensions determine the level at which people will master Sales Skills.

Let us begin with clearly defining the sales skills and look at ways to measure them by screening resumes and using interview questions. We will then look in greater detail at the first three dimensions of the "Best Salesperson Profile" - Attitudes, Motivations and Character.

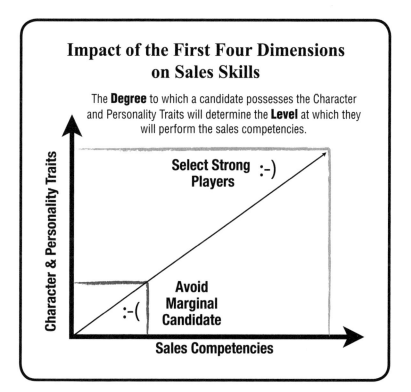

Impact of the First Four Dimensions on Sales Skills

The **Degree** to which a candidate possesses the Character and Personality Traits will determine the **Level** at which they will perform the sales competencies.

Select Strong Players :-)

Avoid Marginal Candidate :-(

Character & Personality Traits

Sales Competencies

Chapter 7:

Measuring Sales Skills on the Resume and During the Interview

Even though "Sales Skills" is the fifth dimension in the "Best Salesperson Profile", it is important that we first have a clear definition of these sales skills before we delve deeper into the other four dimensions. Whether you have an intuitive or in-depth understanding of sales skills, a quick explanation of each of the skills will guarantee we are in agreement on the stages of a best-practice sales process before we talk about how to look for the sales skills.

> As mentioned earlier, the first question that arises is, "Do I hire a person well trained in sales, or do I hire someone who needs sales training?"

As mentioned earlier, the first question that arises is, "Do I hire a person well trained in sales, or do I hire someone who needs sales training?" It all depends on your training resources. i.e. time and ability to train. You be the judge of your own training capabilities and resources.

If you are considering candidates with no sales experience, it is critical to master the skills in the "Recruit the Best" system, since candidates' scores in the other four dimensions will determine the level at which they will master the sales skill. Following a system greatly increases your chances of making a great hiring decision about candidates with no sales experience.

If you are recruiting candidates with sales experience, following are the sales skills they will need. I have included a few sample questions along with the types of answers the best salespeople give during the interview.

Networking and Finding Prospects

Finding enough prospects is the critical first step in all sales positions. If candidates are responsible for finding and generating prospects, they must have a clear understanding of all the ways to source leads. Top salespeople are willing to get out in the community to prospect, and they master the skills necessary to build networking relationships. They get involved in the following: Rotary or other service organizations; networking groups like BNI, eWomen, etc.; Chambers of Commerce, and many ways of creating numerous casual relationships for the purpose of doing business. If not selling in local markets, salespeople must have a strategy on a national level aimed at getting prospects. Great networkers participate in and are good at social networking for the purpose of building an online profile to find prospects and network with existing customers.

Do they get out in the communities and proactively look for prospects? Do they rely on cold calling, or do they join networking groups to find prospects? *(Many people brag about their desire to cold call. Look for their networking desires, abilities and successes versus cold calling desire. I like people who have been in a networking group for three years and are involved in service organizations versus the person who says they make twenty cold calls a day.)*

Have they mastered the skills for prospecting with existing customers? Top salespeople execute the sales process in a professional manner that not only gets the sale, but gains referrals. A great resource for this skill is Bill Cates, "The Referral Coach". Go to his Website at www.ReferralCoach.com and buy his program to master this skill.

Setting Appointments and Holding Appointments

Top salespeople are great at phoning or emailing to set appointments. Phoning skills and strategies to get decision makers on the phone or to open emails are critical. The strength of the referral source determines how hard it is to get appointments with decision makers. The number of set appointments compared to the number of held appointments is a tight ratio for top producers.

Ask candidates to describe their strategy for getting decision makers on the phone and/or to open their emails. Ask them how many phone calls and/or emails they send out on a daily basis, when they perform these activities, and how much time they spend setting appointments. Find out their ratio of phone/email contacts to appointments set. The best salespeople can clearly articulate their strategy, the sales language they use and their success ratios for this sales task.

Fact Finding

The objective of the first meeting with a prospect is to skillfully gain the trust of the prospect and transition the meeting into a fact-finding interview where the salesperson discovers the need for his or her product or service, determines who all the decision makers are, and strategizes the sales process. Great salespeople have the ability to identify the people who have influence in the decision process and know how to get fact-finding meetings with all of them. They also know how to get every decision maker and influencer to the presentation. They are great at controlling the time and pace of the meeting. They skillfully transition the fact-finding meeting into a presentation or schedule the next meeting or series of next-step meetings.

Ask candidates to give you an example of a recent sales situation where it was a challenge to get a meeting with a key prospect. Get them to tell you the story of getting the meeting, gathering the facts, discovering the need, and getting all the decision makers to the presentation. The strength of the story will give you a clear indication of skill level. Make sure they include details of time frames between meetings and milestones in the sales process. After they tell you this story, ask them, "How did you learn those sales skills?"

Making the Presentation

Professional salespeople are highly skilled at making presentations that tie the benefits and features of their product to the needs and pains they uncovered in the fact-finding interview. They know what information to present and in just the right amounts. They understand the importance of presenting, listening for feedback/questions/concerns and involving all the decision makers. They are always prepared with materials and presentations that are specific, not generic, to the needs of the prospect.

The best salespeople always have a direct and professional way of asking for the order. A common way to ask for the order at the end of the presentation is this question, "How do you see this solution working for you?" It is after this question is asked, that the sales process really begins.

Ask candidates to describe the important elements of a strong presentation. They should clearly explain the relationship between their presentation and the needs of the prospect. Their story includes details of the importance of gathering all decision makers, listening to objections/concerns and controlling the presentation to skillfully stay on point.

Sales managers frequently tell me of a technique they use to measure the candidates' presentation skills. They will pick up an ink pen off their desk, hand it to the candidate and say, "Sell me this ink pen." I personally prefer a comprehensive system with processes, tools, and skills that help me make a logical recruiting decision over this type of "cliché" question. The best candidates recognize the difference between the two approaches. A more professional, comprehensive approach to recruiting helps attract the best salespeople and causes the best candidates to view other recruiters as unprofessional. Top salespeople make the connection between a comprehensive selection process verses a recruiting approach that is more random in nature and more focused on selling them on the career.

Handling Fears/Concerns/Objections

The best salespeople have asked the "buying" question. Prospects then begin to ask questions and express concerns. Top salespeople are prepared for all the questions and objections. They have studied their industry, product, customers and competition. They know the top five to ten objections and have strategized very detailed and honest answers to each of the top objections. In confident anticipation, the best salespeople make sure they clearly understand the prospect's fears and concerns about buying. They then masterfully articulate an honest answer that calms any fears the prospect may have had. Mediocre salespeople give random, off the cuff answers to the prospect's questions that lead to distrust.

To determine candidates' skill level in handling objections, ask the candidates to tell you the top five objections they get when making a presentation. Pick one of the objections and tell them to tell you the answer they give to this objection. The best salespeople quickly give you their top five with well thought out and researched answers.

Closing the Sale

Call this step by any number of names—closing the sale, getting the order, or securing a customer. The best salespeople are skillful at staying in the listening and answering loop until all the fears/concerns/questions/objections have been answered. They continue to ask for the order until both parties agree on the appropriate next step. The next best step may or may not be to complete the order. The best salespeople get the main decision makers to tell them the next step. They stay in the listening and advising loop until the prospects make the decision to buy from them. They execute this sales process in such a pleasantly professional manner that prospects buy and recommend them to others.

> It is important to realize which sales skills are the most challenging to execute.

To measure candidates' skills in this step, ask them to tell you their percentage of presentations to orders secured. Ask them to tell you about a recent sale they made to a particularly challenging prospect and how they were able to close the sale. The best salespeople know their metrics and have many great stories of sales almost lost, but finally won because of their skills.

It is important to realize which sales skills are the most challenging to execute. In my sales career, I have discovered that sixty cents of every commission dollar earned comes from these activities: finding enough quality prospects and setting enough first appointments in which I gain enough trust so that the prospect agrees to answer my fact-finding questions. Ten cents of every commission dollar comes from making the presentation. Thirty cents of the commission dollar comes from properly handling the prospects' fears and concerns in a way that I close the sale in a timely manner.

Many people can make a presentation. Very few people are great at getting to the presentation step and closing the sale, which requires great skill in prospecting, getting meetings, handling objections and controlling the sales process. Commission is not paid on the presentation alone. We only get paid for completing all steps in the sales process.

Recruiting the person who is great at the two portions of the sales process that make up ninety cents of the commission dollar is the greatest challenge. We must not let ourselves be charmed by those traits that give a person the ability to make a great presentation. We must sharpen our recruiting skills so we see past the charm to measure the degree to which a candidate can earn the full commission on a regular basis.

Now that we have clearly defined the sales skills and looked at a few ways to discover those skills, let us look at some things the best salespeople do that give further evidence that they can sell your product.

Measuring Sales Experience from the Resume

Look at the resume to see whether or not candidates have similar sales experience to what you want them to do. Is this sales experience in an area of sales where they have performed at their best? Did prospects approach them or did they have to go find prospects? Was the product sales cycle short or long? Was the product tangible or intangible? Was it high-activity or low-activity selling? Was it a high or low rejection environment? How competitive was the product they were selling? Was the product more of a commodity or a product that was easy to sell because of its one-of-a-kind benefits and features? Did the product they were selling require a needs-based sales approach? What kind of formal sales training have they had? What evidence do you see on the resume that they are making an effort to get better? Do they list sales training certification courses?

Other Indicators of Sales Skills During the Interview:

Great salespeople act like salespeople in all areas of their lives, especially during the interview process. Their behavior while you are interviewing them is the same as it will be in their sales calls. I am not referring to the fast-talking "schmoozer". I am talking about salespeople who can back their words up with past performance. Here are some ways we look for evidence that the candidates can sell.

The best salespeople research you and your company.

How well candidates prepare for the interview is a major indicator as to the type of salespeople they are or will become. The first thing they should do is research your company and its career opportunity. They should be prepared to accurately articulate all the ways they will benefit your company. If you have a scheduled face to face or phone interview, and they have not researched your company, the interview should be very short. This is especially the case since the homework step in this system is to research the company prior to the interview.

Early in the process, ask, "What do know about our company?" Look for a well-researched answer. There is a long list of personality traits, character traits and sales skills that this question reveals: Work Ethic, Goal-orientation, and Personal Responsibility, just to name a few. The best salespeople know to do their homework on prospects before they call on them. If they are not going to research a job they are applying for, they are not going to research prospects.

I am always impressed when candidates have taken the time to read my Linkedin profile. The best salespeople take the time to comprehensively research the person who will be interviewing them and can advance their career. The best candidates are smart enough to know that inside information puts them in an advantageous position.

The best salespeople can clearly articulate a "best practice" sales process.

My brother is a master electrician. When I ask him to explain how he fixed the electrical problem that caused the lights in my kitchen to flicker, he can give me a very detailed answer. When I ask candidates who claim to be great salespeople to explain the sales process they use, and they give me their rambling philosophy of why they like selling, I know that they do not followed a best practice process. I like it when the candidates can clearly tell me about the sales process they use and why it works. They quickly recite the basic framework of a face-to-face sales process similar to the one we described earlier. i.e. Prospecting - getting appointments - gathering facts – presenting - handling objections - closing. When candidates describe a best-practice sales process, make sure it matches the process necessary to sell your product?

The best salespeople continue to improve their sales skills.

The great motivational speaker and author Zig Ziglar said, "We are all like fruit. If we are not ripening, we are rotting." Product training, face-to-face sales skills and motivational training are three separate and distinct types of training. The best salespeople are always investing time and money in all three areas. They read books, listen to audio training, attend seminars, hire personal coaches, and attend company conventions. They are always learning and feeding their minds with positive affirmations.

Ask questions like, "What is the name of a sales book you have read?" "Who is your favorite motivational speaker?" "What sales training have you had?" "What are some things you do to stay current with this industry?" The best salespeople do not have to think about this question. They quickly tell you about the authors and speakers they admire. They tell you about the industry publications they read and meetings they attend.

The best salespeople use their sales skills during the interview process.

I use this question to give candidates an opportunity to show me the way they will act in front of an intimidating prospect. I ask, "What do you think of this interview so far?" The best salespeople say things like, "I am enjoying this. It's not much different than a sales call." Salespeople who do well in front of intimidating prospects are calm and confident during a job interview. If they can back up their words with proof of performance, their interview is a time for them to showcase their sales skills.

The best salespeople ask for the job at the end of the interview.

I ask this question at the end of the face-to-face interview to measure candidates' ability to ask for the sale; "What questions do you have for me?" I continue to ask this question, until they say that they do not have any more questions. I am giving them the perfect opportunity to ask me "Do I get the job?" "What is the next step?" Strong salespeople ask for the order. Strong candidates ask for the job in a confident and direct way.

The best salespeople set goals and track critical activities toward reaching goals.

The most productive salespeople understand the importance of goal setting and doing enough of the right activities to reach their goal. They have written income goals with daily activity targets. They use tools to record and compare actual activities against required activities to reach their income goal. I have found that only the most disciplined salespeople use activity-tracking tools. These are usually the top producers on their team. They understand the importance of personal accountability.

During the interview, find out if they have a personal income goal above their quota. Do they know the following sales activity ratios: prospects found to appointments set; appointments held to quotes presented; presentations made to sales obtained? Have they mastered their metrics? *(Knowing the correct ratios is not good enough. Their metrics must be in line with top salespeople in your industry.)* Ask to see the records they keep for setting goals and tracking sales activities. The best salespeople keep and know their stats, just like great baseball players know their batting ratios.

The best salespeople win annual sales awards on a regular basis.

Many salespeople highlight their monthly sales awards on their resumes. I have found that monthly sales awards are a very inaccurate measurement of success. It is a common practice among many salespeople to "sandbag" sales in order to manipulate their sales numbers. Sales results over a twelve-month period compared to the rest of the team can be a more accurate measure of sales performance. Look for this information: How have they stacked up against the rest of their sales team over the last twelve months?

However, always realize that it is possible that you may be passing over someone who has great ability, but has not been in the right environment to succeed. Similarly, a diamond in another environment may be a lump of coal in your company because the conditions under which they thrive are not present.

With the "Recruit the Best" system, you will be able to determine the candidates' true nature and abilities, and not be overly distracted by their past performance alone. The entire system has to do with measuring whether candidates have the traits and personality that will enable them to master these sales skills. The

> **These three elements are mostly developed in our past from the influence of parents, teachers, mentors and our culture.**

higher candidates score in Attitudes, Motivations, Character and Personality, the easier it is for you to determine the level at which they ramp up quickly and begin to be a profitable member of your sales team.

Now that we have a clear understanding of the sales skills that we look for in each candidate, let us turn our attention to looking in greater detail at the first three elements of the "Best Salesperson Profile". These elements, along with Personality Traits, will determine the level at which candidates will master the sales skills: Attitudes, Motivations and Character Traits.

1. Attitudes

2. Motivations

These dimensions are formed in our past.

3. Character

4. Personality

5. Sales Skills

The past may predict the future. Attitudes, Motivations and Character Traits are formed in the past and impact future behaviors.

Let us dig deeper into the first three of the five elements that make up the "Best Salesperson Profile": Attitudes, Motivations and Character Traits. Knowledge improves skills. Understanding how these elements are developed in candidates helps to improve our interviewing skills. These three elements are mostly developed in our past from the influence of parents, teachers, mentors and our culture. It requires a constant daily effort to continue to grow in these three areas, but the most successful candidates have a strong foundation. This foundation is built in the past.

We measure the strength of this foundation in order to help us predict future performance. The foundation is built from exposure to training and mentoring. We must measure the degree to which candidates have been exposed to these important areas of influence. How much have they been exposed to the character traits? What is it that causes them to be motivated to work with the products and services you are currently selling? What in their life causes them to need money? What in their current situation do they want to change and make better?

The foundation of character is built in the following manner. In order for a character trait to be present in large amounts, it must be imprinting on the individual at an early age. The degree to which a trait is imprinted depends upon our having had specific impactful experiences. A parent gives an instruction, and we either obey or disobey. If we disobey, our parent is there on a consistent basis correcting the behavior. We experience a sense of authority over us. We experience the satisfaction of compliance. We learn there are negative consequences to bad behavior and positive consequences to good behavior. We learn that when we choose the path that goes against instruction, we hurt others and ourselves.

We learn that when we obey, we experience gratification for a job well done. This sense of gratification causes us to want to echo, or choose to repeat, the positive behavior. During this moment of alignment of praise and gratification, we experience a bonding to the parent and the character trait. This bonding grows each time the alignment occurs. In both situations of punishment and praise, there is an emotional experience. The accumulation of these emotional experiences, over time, determines the degree to which we possess a character trait.

This process resembles the creation of a ceramic vessel. A skilled potter begins with soft clay, and manipulates it to the desired shape and function. It is then fired to 1400 degrees. A glass-forming glaze is then applied, then more heat. This time, it is fired to over 2000 degrees to form a protective glass coating on the vessel. This process requires a great deal of expertise to form the vessel and a special mixture of ingredients to form the glaze. After many hours in the high heat, and after a slow cooling and curing process, a beautiful work of art emerges.

Productive patterns of the past are formed when corrective instruction (heat) comes from a reliable teacher. We put the teaching into practice while under more heat and pressure. Under the right kind of mentoring, this process is repeated over many years, and we grow and mature and naturally seek the path of high character.

The "Recruit the Best" system helps us to discover the areas of candidates' lives that have been through the refining process, as well as those areas that have not. We are looking for candidates with many refined patterns of productivity. There are no perfect people, but you want someone with a past who experienced teachers, mentors and trainers in all these important areas. After filling out the "Matching Score Sheet", you may decide to hire candidates knowing they may not have been exposed to all you would like for them to have learned. By following this process, you will know what areas to train and refine through proper coaching.

Now that we know how the foundation of Attitudes, Motivations and Character is built, let us look at each element in greater detail and also look at how to use interview questions to measure the degree to which candidates have each element.

Chapter 8:

Critical Attitudes of the Best Salespeople

Almost any psychologist will tell you that our belief about ourselves determines our behavior. They will also tell us that honest people have a hard time performing job duties that are not aligned with their values. Based on these two psychological facts, there are two critical attitudes of the best salespeople on which we want to focus. The first is the attitude of candidates toward salespeople. The other is the attitude of candidates toward using your products and services to solve the problems of your customers.

> The first is the attitude of candidates toward salespeople. The other is the attitude of candidates toward using your products and services to solve the problems of your customers.

Do candidates see salespeople as generally worthy of respect, helpful, and deserving of success? What are the things in the candidates' lives that cause them to have a positive or negative view of salespeople? Have candidates had personal and meaningful experiences in their lives that cause them to view your products and services in a positive light?

Much of the groundwork for our attitudes has been laid in our past. I remember, as a child, that on a regular basis, a man drove up to our house in a big shiny new Cadillac. It was beautiful. The salesman sat at our kitchen table and talked to my mom, and she gave him money. I watched this scenario many times as I grew up. The first time I saw him, I was impressed with his car, his suit and his air of importance. I later learned that he was in financial services sales, and the critical role his company's products would play if my dad died. I was thankful for his services. I wanted a career like that. I also watched my uncle have a successful career selling financial services for over forty years. That further encouraged me to pursue a career in sales, and developed my view of salespeople as respected, important and successful.

Strong candidates have similar stories and tell them with passion during the interview process. Steer clear of do-it-yourselfers who do not feel they need salespeople. They are unlikely to be able to convince your customers that salespeople are a necessary part of the equation if they do not truly believe it themselves.

Furthermore, listen carefully to screen out those who are just "trying" sales on their way to another career or until their "dream job" comes along. You want to accurately measure their attitudes toward your product or service. A strong passion for your product and service will help them survive the rejection and even disrespectful treatment by prospects as they build customers who value their services and expertise.

Uncovering Attitudes

We have an entire field manual with the interview questions needed to discover all the traits and competencies in the "Best

Sales Person Profile". You can find it on our website, CanTheySell. com. For now, let us look at a few questions that would enable you to uncover candidates' attitudes toward your product or service, and sales as a career. Notice that the sample questions below are all open-ended questions that encourage the candidates to open up and tell you their stories:

- Tell me about a time when you bought a product like we sell.

- Describe the decision-making process you went through.

- If you needed our product today, what is it about our product that would cause you to purchase it over our competitor's product?

- When you hear the word, "salesperson", what first comes to your mind?

- How do you see yourself in comparison to that description?

- Why do you think I am asking you these questions?

The first words out of the candidates' mouths will generally give you a pretty good idea of their true attitude about sales and selling. Are their answers quick and concise or do their answers sound made up and contrived?

Negative attitudes toward salespeople may show up in candidates' history of inconsistent achievement of sales awards over time. A red flag is also raised if they have jumped around among sales, management, and operations departments. Ask more questions if they have consistently been in low-pressure situations such as customer service or retail selling, versus the type of selling you need for them to do. If your compensation is mostly commission based, look for commission sales positions versus mostly salaried positions. Have they achieved consistency and growth in earning commissions?

Too many sales managers start with asking or trying to determine if a person can sell. They may or may not have sales skills, but if they do not have a good image of themselves as a salesperson, they cannot be successful in the long run. Their self-image will not allow it.

I see this scenario all the time. Candidates like a product—for example, investment services - but when I start talking to them about the product, they have bought all their investments online, bypassing interaction with a salesperson. They love the product and purchase on a regular basis, but they have never trusted a salesperson to give them advice. They do not rely on salespeople as a trusted advisor with any product they buy. How, in turn, can you expect them to *be* that trusted person when they do not trust other salespeople in making their own purchases? Pretty soon in the interview, they realize, "Gee, I seem to avoid salespeople." They may love the product, but their negative image of salespeople will prevent them from surviving in a sales career.

Do they see themselves as professional salespeople? *(The best salespeople are not just passing through a sales job on their way to the job they really dream about. Weak salespeople are good at getting the job and milking your base salary and moving on to the next sales manager victim.)*

Some sales managers make the mistake of assuming that something on a resume is evidence of the right attitude or skill set they need. Remember that just because people have been leaders in a sorority or fraternity does not mean they can sell. Just because they once ran their own company does not mean they can sell. The fact that someone was once a star athlete does not mean he can sell. The fact candidates were once successful at something else, does not mean they can sell. You want to ask about their success stories. Was it primarily through their own efforts that the team was successful, or were they just a part of the right team at the right time? Exactly what part did they play in making it happen? What are all the factors of their success story, and most importantly, do they translate to being able to sell in a high-activity, high-rejection sales environment?

You are looking for salespeople who can create something from nothing. You want salespeople who can find prospects, get appointments, gain permission to ask questions about the prospect's needs, and then give a presentation that causes the prospect to buy. Executing the sales process in a confident and efficient manner is totally different from leading a company or playing a subordinate role on a team.

What evidence is in your candidates' past that indicates they can sell your type of product? Is there also evidence in their past or from your interview that they enjoy selling and are good at it? Can they do it over and over all day long and stick with it when it gets hard? What evidence is in their past of a passion for solving the problems of people using your product? Honest salespeople have a sincere desire to make life better for their customers. The product they sell is simply the tool for making things better.

The best evidence of this passion is their ownership and use of the product they sell. For example, great financial services and insurance salespeople have a passion for helping people wade through the complexities of products and life's financial problems to save for the future and protect against the unexpected. Top salespeople who sell office equipment, cellular phones, computers, etc., all have a story about why they love solving problems by using the product they sell. And they give you passionate reasons they personally own the products they sell to others.

Any candidates who cannot articulate with emotion why they are passionate about your product do not have the attitude toward your product necessary to be a long-term member of your team.

Asking the following questions can help you uncover the candidates' attitude toward your product or service:

- "What do you know about us and like about what we do?" *You are looking for words like "strong company", "leader in your industry", "help people solve major issues with...", "I like helping people with the challenge of.... and using your product to solve this challenge."*

- "What caused you to have an interest in this job with us?" *You are looking for words like "customer of your company", "like your product and the problems it solves", likes to sell/serve, advancement, commission driven...".*

- "What has been your experience in dealing with salespeople in our industry and owning similar products?" *You are looking for positive words about salespeople in your industry and purchasing from salespeople, not over the Internet.*

Chapter 9:

Motivating Factors Transport You Through the Sweat Zone

Now that candidates have passed the "Attitudes" test, it is time to see if they have the right motivations to be successful. Many different things motivate people to move forward in their lives. I have found that the best salespeople have some common motivating factors that drive them to succeed. Let us look at those factors.

Salespeople need to have enough personal financial needs to keep them working through what I call the "Sweat Zone". They need a reason to make calls when it gets hard, and keep pressing through whether they feel like it or not. Salespeople with financial needs and a desire for a better future will keep going under difficult circumstances. Having goals for a better future gives you an indication about how mature they are in their ability to think about the future and provide for it.

You want salespeople who are sufficiently motivated. Usually this means salespeople who are financially responsible for one or more people in addition to themselves, whether that is children or a spouse or an entire family—being financially responsible is good and motivating. Getting out of debt is another motivating factor, although you do not want salespeople who are so desperate for money that they cannot think straight or concentrate on the job at hand. The best salespeople go to work every day because they are motivated to meet their immediate financial, physical and spiritual needs. Once immediate needs are met, they set goals for making a better future for themselves and others. Mature people focus on future needs. Everyone has immediate needs.

To screen for motivations, we want to measure the immediate and future financial, physical and spiritual needs that can be met if salespeople perform well in this job. We want their needs and future desires to be in line with the job opportunities, and we want to make sure they are "doers" and not just dreamers.

Examples of immediate needs might be to understand and improve upon relationships or to increase strength of character. Immediate financial needs might include personal and family care. Financial needs include providing for contingencies for a spouse such as life, disability, long term care insurance, investments, savings and debt reduction. More long-term financial goals might include education for children; home purchase; care for extended family; or retirement funding. Physical goals might include improving their working environment, diet or health. Longer-term goals might include community projects or, changing something in the world, or otherwise making a larger difference in others' lives.

Evidence of a candidate's sufficient level of motivation on a resume would include a history of job changes that have resulted in progressive advancement and income growth, and a resume objective that uses words like advancement, opportunity and growth.

If candidates cannot articulate their financial and/or physical motivations, pass them by. If they can live on $65,000 a year, they are not likely to push to do well in a $120,000 a year sales job.

They are going to be satisfied with much less. You want sales-people who will keep going when the going gets tough, because they are motivated by outside circumstances, such as family responsibilities, or motivated internally through a constant drive for improvement. These are salespeople who set goals, reach them, and set more goals.

When screening for appropriate motivations, ask, "What in your current financial situation would you be able to satisfy if you got this position?" You want to make sure they are making the connection between what they want, and how to make it happen in this company. Very few managers measure the connection between the candidates' needs and the amount of money the candidates must earn.

To measure income needs, ask, "What is the minimum amount of money you need to earn?" Look for an income that is close to the higher end of base salary plus potential commission for the position you have open. When answering this question, candidates had better have a number in mind, not just what they think may fit into your budget. You do not want someone who can live on half of what this job pays. Detriments are spouses with high earnings, or salespeople who want to be busy but do not need to work, or who are working to feel

> The truth is, we live in a world that is constantly falling to pieces. So if we are not growing, we are going to decay. We want someone who is always driven to make it better, no matter how good it gets.

"fulfilled." They need to be doing it because they are a "fit" for the position and they need the money, plain and simple. They have financial needs and goals that will take all or most of their earnings. Do not make the mistake of getting excited about hiring candidates who give you a low target income. I have seen too many managers think, "Well, I can get this person for much less than I anticipated."

Most recruiters start the selection process by looking at sales skills and skip Attitudes and Motivations. You can have salespeople with great sales skills, but if they do not have something in their lives they want to change, they are not likely to apply those skills well or consistently. If they do not have something they want to change, they likely do not have any goals. If attitudes and motivations are not there, I do not really care about going further with my interview. They just do not need this job badly enough.

The truth is, we live in a world that is constantly falling to pieces. So if we are not growing, we are going to decay. We want someone who is always driven to make it better, no matter how good it gets. We want salespeople who understand that the state they are in today, left unattended, will get worse automatically. So they have got to make it better, or weeds will grow. They understand, "If it is to be, it is up to me." And they are never satisfied with mediocrity.

One good way to encourage candidates to reveal their motivations is to ask, "What are the three most important things in your life right now?" I have to thank my partner, Lance Cooper, for teaching me this question. It is brilliant. In terms of answers, I like it when one of their top three answers includes having someone else to take care of. This answer shows they are concerned about someone outside of themselves. Another good answer to this question relates to having a moral center. This shows they are not just making up their own rules in life. I also want to hear about their career somewhere in that list. Occasionally, I have people who do not list their career as being in the top three, and I have passed them by. Their motivation to succeed in a high-activity sales environment was not sufficient for them to be successful in the job I had available.

Chapter 10:

Measuring Character

Using the "Recruit the Best" system, we measure the five dimensions in the "Best Salesperson Profile". We first make sure candidates have sufficient amounts of Attitudes and Motivations. We then score candidates in the critical Character Traits of Concern for Others, Honesty, Work Ethic, and Responsibility. Then, we use the science of the Craft Personality Questionnaire to determine their personality traits. After we have a good measure of character traits and personality traits, we can then look at these two sets of traits in combination. Studying these combination traits gives us in-depth information needed to predict future behavior of candidates. The tools and processes inside the "Recruit the Best" system that give us this in-depth information are benefits of the system that set it apart from other ways of recruiting.

> The tools and processes inside the "Recruit the Best" system that give us this in-depth information are benefits of the system that set it apart from other ways of recruiting.

As an employer, you will have very minimal influence on character, so your team members must bring strong character with them to the job. This is why you want to hire character first. You measure character traits using interviewing techniques as well as questionnaires that are available in the field manual for *Can They Sell* at CanTheySell.com

Remember, we are born selfish. We spend our lives learning to suppress this root of selfishness and pride. If you have any doubt of that, spend some time with a two-year-old. The favorite words of a two-year-old are typically "mine" and "I want ..." It is reputed that a great philosopher once said that we are born selfish, and the only reason a baby does not strangle its mother for its milk is because its arms are too short and too uncoordinated. Strong character is never a destination, but a daily journey of making difficult choices each time life presents its challenges.

The harder we work to suppress our selfish desires, the easier it becomes to exercise the Character traits. The more we seek to satisfy our selfish desires, the harder it becomes to exercise high Character.

Mature character and strength to suppress selfishness comes from wisdom learned from our mistakes, advice offered from trusted others, and the exercise of discipline when faced with hard choices. Spiritual training and commitment also contribute to our ability to live beyond our own selfish desires. The more we exercise a character trait and experience positive results, the more that trait becomes a part of our character. Psychologists tell us that a majority of our character traits are imprinted on us as early as age five. Motivational speaker and author Dr. Denis Waitley once said that most of our self-image is imprinted by age five, and then we spend the next 70 years getting over it!

Your job in the interview process is to discover the level at which candidates experienced these emotional connections. This

Well-developed Character Makes it Easier to Supress Our Natural Selfishness

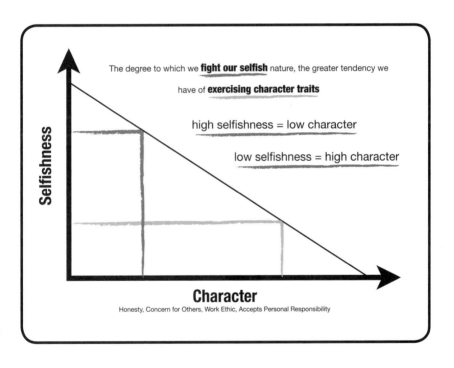

The degree to which we **fight our selfish** nature, the greater tendency we have of **exercising character traits**

high selfishness = low character

low selfishness = high character

Selfishness

Character
Honesty, Concern for Others, Work Ethic, Accepts Personal Responsibility

task is really much easier than it sounds. If you know the right questions, you simply ask until you can get them to open up about their character-building experiences. Candidates' stories give evidence of mentors who have had an impact on their character. Stories of failures and successes show areas of maturity and wisdom. Recent successes will show the level of character they will bring when they join your team. They also talk about the books they are reading and things they are doing to grow personally - things like working with a personal coach, pursuing spiritual growth or meeting with a mentor show they are growing emotionally and professionally.

As we mentioned earlier, character is determined by training and mentoring early in life, and personality is hard-wired from birth. We will talk about each of the four character traits individually, and later go over what they mean in combination with the personality traits.

Character Trait #1: Honesty

In its simplest form, Honesty is living and speaking the truth to yourself and others. Yet, when I talk about Honesty, people tell me it is the hardest trait to discern. We live in a culture that increasingly believes that truth is relative rather than absolute. I think everyone would agree that we want to hire salespeople with the same level of Honesty that we expect from any salesperson from whom we purchase.

I have always found it ironic that people do not want others to lie to them but they are often willing to lie to others. Honesty is one trait that we impose on others to a greater degree than we are willing to exercise ourselves. White lies, or "spin", it is really pretty black and white.

Let us first look at how Honesty is developed. It starts with training in absolute truth and in right and wrong. Those people who have not had that parent or mentor who has instilled Honesty in them from the beginning are always going to struggle with honesty. If they cannot remember the first time they felt the weight of guilt for lying, then maybe they have not experienced that training. Honesty is learned when the desire for a clean conscience outweighs the feelings of guilt and disappointment. Honest people are strong enough to deal with whatever challenges are brought about from telling the truth.

I remember giving my Honesty muscle a workout. Unfortunately, I remember too well a lie I told my mother. It had to do with avoiding homework in order to play outside on a beautiful fall day. On the school bus ride home, I made a commitment to myself to quickly finish my homework so I could play outside. I jumped off the bus, removed my shoes and began to enjoy the cool ground on my toes as I headed toward the house to complete my homework. The smell in the air, the cool ground and the warmth outside were intoxicating.

When I entered the house, Mom asked her usual question, "Do you have any homework?" Now eager to be outside, I replied with a convincing, "No, I finished it on the bus." She was pleased and sent me out to play. Within the first five minutes, I saw my beautiful mother's smile from the kitchen window as she mouthed the words, "I love you." All of a sudden, for maybe the first time in my life, I began to understand the emotions of a guilty conscience. These feelings began to override my sensation of freedom. The rest of my playtime was spoiled as I struggled, but failed, to regain those feelings of joy. I was miserable until finally admitting that I had lied. Even at a young age, I saw the impact lying had on relationships and the damage it did to a clean conscience.

When we experience the negative consequences and burden of a guilty conscience caused by dishonesty, and choose the comfort of a clear conscience over the temporary ease of dishonesty, we become bonded to the trait of Honesty. How do you find out if your candidates have had this experience?

There are evidences of dishonesty in candidates. Look for exaggerations on their resume. When we get to personality traits, you may find that those who have high scores on the Good Impression trait on the Craft Personality Questionnaire might struggle with exaggerating when describing their strengths and weaknesses. I am concerned about candidates' honesty when I ask them about their weaknesses, and they pause for a moment, pondering their answer, then blurt out, "I am impatient with lazy people." They may also say, "I am a workaholic." These are, in fact, strengths. These attempts to take a strength and state it as a weakness cause me to question their Honesty.

A lack of Honesty in salespeople will not only put your relationships with your customers at risk, but will also negatively impact the sales team as a whole. You will find that dishonest people will over-promise and under-deliver to everyone. These individuals are generally undependable, and cannot be trusted to deliver on their promises. (Dependability is a combination of high Work Ethic and Honesty.) You will also find that people who struggle with Honesty may gossip where they speak negatively about another person who is not present. Lying to customers and coworkers will kill your business like a fast-growing cancer. It can have a major negative impact on your personal brand as well as the company brand.

First, screen for evidence of dishonesty on the resume, and follow up with your interview questions. This typically comes out when people list the accomplishments +participation may have been minimal. A lot of people will do the least amount of work necessary to be able to list it on their resume. To reveal whether or not this is the case, listen for the word "I" versus the word "we" when they tell the story.

You find whether Honesty exists in the way a person tells a story. Here are two different stories from actual interviews I had on the same day that clearly illustrate this point. The first story tells of a candidate who was modest, but honest. The second story tells of a candidate who exaggerated when describing the specific role in the task.

> *The first interview was with a candidate who told me about finding several million dollars of grant money available for his school. He went with a team to D.C., met with a senator, put together a proposal, and got the money. The first time he told the story, he used the word "we" all the way through it. I asked him to please tell me the story again, and use the word "I". He told the story again, which revealed that he had been very modest about his part in the process. He said, "I discovered the money was available, I put together a team, I contacted the senator, put the proposal together, and we got the grant money." He had other people helping him, but had obviously done most of the work himself.*

> *Another candidate had been in a sorority in college. She told me about raising a lot of money for charity while on a fundraising committee. I asked her, as I had the gentleman above, to tell me again, using the word "I." She began by saying, "I was involved in raising money for charity, and we ... and we ... and we ... " So she had not really been a leader, but had just participated as they raised money. She had a very hard time articulating what her part had been.*

As mentioned earlier, indicators of dishonesty are monthly sales awards listed on the resume that only happen once or twice in a twelve-month period. It is easy to "sandbag" one month and win the next. I want to know if salespeople have won an annual award and how their annual sales stack up against those of other team members.

Get to the real truth of why they have left other jobs. A lot of people job-hop and present it as "well rounded, multi-disciplined experience in a variety of fields." To find out why they left, ask this question, "When I call and ask your boss why you left, what will he tell me?"

You will also see people round up their GPA, when a 2.7 becomes a 3.0. They also may exaggerate job accomplishments or responsibilities. Some will say they coached salespeople when the truth is they ran the sales meeting a few times when the boss was away. So ask questions carefully about what is on their resume. Begin screening from the very first phone call for Attitudes, Motivations and Character. Ask the following questions. These may seem to be pretty straightforward questions, but you can never assume that a person is going to answer an interview question a certain way.

- What would you do if our products or services are not what a prospect needs or wants? *(I have actually had people tell me that they would find a way to sell it to the prospect anyway. They think that is what I want to hear, of course, but it reveals a great deal about their character, and not in a good way.)*

- Which of these traits is the most important one for the type of sales we do - Persistence, Self-Discipline, Honesty, or Work Ethic? *(You might think candidates all answer "Honesty." But they do not.)*

- When I speak to your last boss, what will he tell me are your greatest strengths and weaknesses? *(If you are having a hard time getting to the truth with a candidate, this question will typically get you the answers you are looking for.)*

Honesty can be a difficult trait to measure. It takes intuition, listening skills and a lot of discernment, but a candidate's resume and great interview questions, along with the personality assessment, are the best tools to work with.

References are a great source for measuring honesty. If candidates struggle with coming up with six references, I question their credibility. While speaking to a reference source, I will pull a sort of "Colombo". By that I mean, while talking to the reference source, out of the blue, I will suddenly ask, "Oh, just one more thing. Can you trust everything Rick says?" When you spring a question like that on someone right in the middle of the conversation, usually the first thing out of their mouth is the truth. "Um ..." means probably not.

Character Trait #2: Concern for Others

As a salesperson, I always appreciate professional help from other great salespeople. It is always a pleasant experience when salespeople greet you warmly, ask questions about your frustrations, and then use their great product knowledge to help you feel good about investing in their product or service. When I need a piece of equipment for my recording studio, I always go to the Guitar Center. This company has done a great job in hiring musicians and tech-savvy people who use the equipment they sell. It is always a great experience. Rather than spending hours researching on the Internet, thinking I might save a few bucks, and waiting days to get my product, I drive down the street to a trusted and knowledgeable source. I then tell all my friends about the excellent service. The salespeople at the Guitar Center are concerned about my needs.

My office is located in an area that attracts salespeople who spend their day cold calling. Over the past four years, I have not taken more than two to three minutes with each these salespeople. They all do the same thing. They barge into my office, flip out their card and begin to up-chuck product information as if I were sitting at my desk in need of the exact product they are selling. The moment a salesperson walks in, apologizes for the interruption, asks me if I have a moment to speak, then begins to ask questions about me and my frustrations, I will most likely buy from him whether I need the product or not. We all respond more positively to people who show a concern for us.

When salespeople immediately show they have our best interest in mind, and not their own, all of our guards come down and
we become open to learning about their product or service. We
then tell all our friends about this professional salesperson.

The character trait of Concern for Others is simply the
"Golden Rule" - *Do unto others as you would have them do unto
you.* While even the Bible tells us to love others as we love ourselves, remember that all of us are born with selfish traits. The
degree to which we can suppress that natural selfish urge, or root,
is the degree to which we will care for others.

The level of this trait in candidates goes back to training
received from parents and mentors. I have also found those with
a higher amount of emotional and spiritual maturity have a greater
Concern for Others. It takes a lot of energy to exercise this trait,
so the less emotional baggage we have, the more we can be free
to show Concern for Others. The psychologist, Dr. Denis Waitley,
says that we can only give away love and Concern for Others to the
degree that we love ourselves. A positive self-image has a lot to do
with the way we treat others. This fact is why it is important that
we all spend time working on our emotional and spiritual maturity.

It helps if our lives are filled with people who have shown a
mentoring interest in us and have helped us get beyond our own
struggles. We all need to regularly spend time reading and listening to positive messages that help us get beyond the emotional
baggage that bogs us down in our own self pity. We are more
likely to want to "pay it forward" and pass on the same help and
support that has been offered to us.

We are all beating a path to something, but the question we
want to have candidates answer is - does the path lead to anything
outside of their own self-interests?

Concern for Others correlates with the personality trait of
Need to Nurture. If a person has a personality with a low Need

to Nurture, it naturally takes more energy to show a Concern for Others, but with the right training early on in life, there is a higher motivation to help others. For people who score high on the personality trait of Need to Nurture, it may take less energy for them to show Concern for Others, but they may also be tempted to get over-involved.

To try to find out the level of their Concern for Others, ask, "What are the three most important things in your life?" Do the candidates spend time outside of work doing something for others? Ask about their level of involvement. Screen out those who just have items on their resumes as window dressing. Look for true involvement in community service, or club memberships that have a service orientation. A person's involvement with his or her family is also a good indicator of concern for other people.

When salespeople have not developed a Concern for Others, they can have a strong negative effect on your whole sales team. They will be slow to follow up when solving customer issues. They will incorrectly recommend products, due to failure to take the time to properly diagnose needs. They may have low productivity due to a lack of financial motivation to take care of themselves or others for whom they are responsible. People who have not developed this Concern for Others tend to criticize easily and put people down. They depersonalize everyone into a rival. They tend to have an insatiable desire to consume without balancing it out with contribution. They tend to have uncontrolled tempers, shallow relationships, addictions, and an inability to live in community with others. Again, emotional baggage will prevent someone from showing Concern for Others.

Character Trait #3: Work Ethic

A person with a strong Work Ethic knows what the goal is, knows what the important tasks are, knows the deadline, then uses a high level of self-discipline to finish the tasks on time. Logic and discipline determine the priorities and deadlines, not emotions. Work Ethic is more about productivity than how hard someone works. If I can teach recruiters where Work Ethic comes from, then they can look for it better, and recognize it and nurture it in others.

Work Ethic was something I learned on the farm in the 1970s. As I mentioned earlier, I was one of five children, and we were all tired at the end of the day, but it was a good kind of tired. Winters were cold, but at suppertime, we ate well. We understood the meaning behind Mom's wisdom when she said, "You cannot wait until you feel good to work. You have to work so you will feel good."

There was a rhythm on the farm of consistent, honest work. There were no short cuts. Mom made sure all five of us contributed our part. If one of us slacked, we all suffered. So, too, if one of your salespeople slacks, the entire team suffers.

When it comes to Work Ethic, there are three types of workers:

1. *Casual Workers* – They enter the door just in time, and appear to be interested in being productive, but have just now begun to think about their to-do list. Allowing their emotions to guide them, they begin to prioritize the list. Like slow burning, wet firewood, over the next hour and a half, they ease into the mood of more challenging tasks. The two hours of focus require a time of ramping down to lunch. After lunch, the cold-molasses pace of expending energy is repeated just in time to go home by five. Inside, they have a good feeling that they were productive based

on the number of hours spent on work-related duties, even though very few or no results were produced.

2. *Counterfeit Workers* - When the boss is around, the counterfeit workers get busy. Time and effort is spent strategizing to be noticed and playing political games. Taking credit for other people's work is their mode of operation. While they talk a good game and schmooze the right people, they know in their hearts they are cheaters; but they also believe cheating is the only way to get ahead.

3. *Committed Workers* - Understanding the balance between work and family is important to the committed workers. Career advancement and job longevity are linked to focusing on serving others. Instead of maneuvering for promotions, they take on responsibilities as a way to contribute to the overall team goal. They work hard, even when they do not feel like working. When at work, they are totally focused only on productive tasks. Understanding their own strengths and weaknesses, they surround themselves with talented people. They get plenty of rest and work to stay physically, emotionally and spiritually fit.

Obviously, you want a committed worker. But, how do you know who is a committed worker? Ask questions. Begin by asking for candidates' definition of Work Ethic. Next ask, "Who taught you that, and how did they teach you?" What you want to hear from those candidates is that they had someone at a young age who told them a job needed to be done, taught them, supervised them while they did the work and checked on their work until they did it right. You also want to hear that a deadline was given, and they were held accountable to those deadlines with quality work. You also want to listen for indications that their training was done with positive reinforcement rather than negative consequences.

In my case, in addition to my mother's teaching, my dad set the example for good Work Ethic. He got up at 5:30 every morning, went to work, got home at 5:00, and then went out and worked in the garden and performed other important chores.

Although I have found success in things like sports, education, music, etc. not to be necessarily good indicators of mastering sales skills, I do find success in these areas to be a good indicator of Work Ethic. One of the best salespeople I ever met was a concert saxophonist. Someone showed him how he could take the same Work Ethic and discipline from musical achievement and apply it to sales. He became very successful.

Candidates show Work Ethic when they customize a cover letter with their resume and customize the "Objective" on the resume to fit the job for which they are applying. Other evidences of hard Work Ethic on a resume include a stable work history with the same company for an extended period of time. Job changes are related to movement upward, and there are many awards for achievement. They will use words or terms like hard work, discipline, achievement and putting in long hours. They will have worked to pay for all or part of their education.

After looking at thousands of resumes, I continue to be shocked at how many people do not get help with writing and/ or editing their resume. I always have to be cautious and look for exaggerations, but I have come to the conclusion that it shows Work Ethic when a person gets help with their resume.

I was mentoring a young man recently who said he wanted to change companies because he felt that opportunity at his present company was simply not there. I suggested that he do research to find the vertical market he desired, then focus on a specific company in that market, research the company and develop some ideas to help the company in a challenging economy. I told him that if he showed he really had some great ideas, it was likely that a company would hire him even if the company were not necessarily recruiting for a salesperson at the time. I know I would be amazed if someone came in my office and showed such initiative. The young man reported back a few weeks later. He actually took my advice but in a different way. He applied the advice to his current job, and is now at the top of his sales team.

The effect of inadvertently hiring someone with low Work Ethic is that it impacts the company by: wasted training dollars, low profits, and low sales bonuses. Other hard working team members must pick up the slack, leading to low team morale.

Character Trait #4: Accepting Personal Responsibility for Outcomes of Your Choices

We accept Personal Responsibility for the outcomes of our choices when we believe that the struggles as well as the accomplishments in our lives are impacted by our choices.

We set our selfish interests aside and realize there is a cause and effect associated with every decision we make. If we have a high maturity level in this character trait, we believe that all our decisions have either a positive or negative impact on ourselves and others. On the positive side, if we want to make something better, it is up to us to take action. On the negative side, if our decision caused a problem, we either choose to admit that we caused the problem, and take action to fix it, or we take our punishment and move on. We do not blame others or make excuses for our mistakes.

Taking Responsibility involves being introspective enough, to ask, "What did I do wrong and what could I have done differently to have caused a better outcome?" Jim Collins, in his book *Good to Great,* refers to this concept as looking in the mirror and changing ourselves, versus looking out the window for someone else to blame. Not being willing to take Responsibility for one's actions and the outcomes from those actions is a character flaw as old as mankind. It is at the heart of the oldest recorded story in history, the one that took place in the Garden of Eden. Instead of accepting responsibility for eating the forbidden fruit, Eve blamed the serpent, and Adam blamed God for giving him Eve.

Not accepting Responsibility is actually a first cousin to lying. We have to be trained to see and practice taking Responsibility. Training starts early. When people bail us out rather than letting us suffer the consequences of bad decisions, learning to take Responsibility becomes difficult. We grow when we begin to favor the desire of a clear conscious over temptation to shirk Responsibility. When we learn to look back and analyze the past in order to grow, we have matured and can move forward. Those who are unwilling to look back are declining rather than growing. Is the candidate you are considering on a growth or declining pattern?

Those of us who take Responsibility for our actions understand freedom of choice. The problem, however, is that most of our challenges come from how this freedom of choice is exercised. We are free to choose the way we feel, regardless of our circumstances. This plays out in sales when we realize we can choose not to feel rejected. We, individually, have the sole power to change the way we feel and react to the circumstances we face. Surrounding ourselves with mentors and personal coaches will help us to make better choices and deal with the consequences of bad ones.

When looking for evidence that candidates have a well-developed sense of Responsibility for their actions, listen as they talk of former companies. If they tell you about leaving several jobs due to the way they were treated by others, or due to companies going out of business, or due to broken promises, stop them and ask, "As you hear yourself tell me about your previous jobs, what do you think I am thinking?" It takes a few tries, but the candidates usually acknowledge that they are not very good at choosing the places they picked to work. The reality is that they failed to perform the due diligence prior to taking their last several jobs. This scenario shows me lack of Personal Responsibility for not acknowledging why they left each job and a lack of Work Ethic for not better researching the company.

These additional interview questions also help you measure the presence of Personal Responsibility.

- Tell me about a time in your life when someone gave you a task that did not work out well.

- What happened, and what could you have done differently? *(Mature candidates spend more time admitting their mistakes and talking about the wrong choices they made versus blaming others for their mistakes.)*

- What are you doing to improve your Sales Skills? What are you doing personally and professionally to grow? *(Mature candidates realize they must take Responsibility for their own moral and professional growth. They are regularly growing by reading, studying and attending training.)*

This concludes the section on essential Character Traits in the "Best Salesperson Profile", and how to screen for them individually. Remember, character is taught at a young age. However, it can be learned later on in life, but is much harder as the years pass.

Personality, on the other hand, is hard-wired into our DNA at birth. We can learn to *manage* our natural tendencies, but they never really change over our lifetimes. The degree to which we must manage our natural personality traits to "fit in" with our job, or our environment, will determine how energy-draining or energy-lifting the activity is for us.

After we go over the Personality Traits individually, we will re-visit the area of Character Traits and talk about various combinations of Character Traits and Personality Traits that are powerful or have built-in trouble.

Thankfully, at one point in my own life, I was forced to face reality about my Character Traits. During a time when I was considering a career change, I was faced with the realization that my current level of character would not be helped by changing jobs, getting another spouse, moving to another city, etc. I was initially mired down in the thinking that my current situation was causing my behavior in treating people poorly and floundering when I should be focused. I realized that I must first change my Character Traits. I must change, grow and create success at the maximum level in the current situation. Otherwise, I will take the same emotional baggage that I currently possess into the new situation, and over time, create the same struggles and challenges that exist today.

I realized the prescription was not to change the situation I was in, but to change the person in the situation. It was up to me to bring strong Character Traits into every job, relationship and interaction and take the responsibility for making things better rather than relying on others to create an environment that pleased me.

As you are recruiting new salespeople, make sure they are not running from something. Make sure they are growing and maturing and getting rid of their emotional challenges instead of bringing it into your company where they will eventually negatively impact your culture.

Part III:

Screening and Measuring Personality Traits–Using Science to Measure Capacity to Master Sales Skills

Behavioral scientists have unlocked the secrets to understanding a person's makeup in terms of personality profiles. While recruiting salespeople, at Sales Manage Solutions we like to use the Craft Personality Questionnaire™ (CPQ®), originally developed by Dr. Larry L. Craft about 35 years ago. Control of the questionnaire is currently owned by the SHL Group Ltd. It is available through our website, CraftProfiles.com.

There are a large variety of personality assessments available to be used while hiring salespeople. The difference among them is in the reporting and data that comes back to you about a potential candidate. That is where we feel the CPQ really shines.

Prior to creating the CPQ, Dr. Craft was a salesperson and in sales management. He then earned his doctorate in Educational Leadership with a focus on Personality Assessments. These years of real world sales experiences gave him incredible insight into the needs and characteristics that sales team leaders are looking for when hiring salespeople. Because of this insight, the information you receive is detailed enough to offer you concrete help in making great hiring decisions. It improves your odds of predicting mastery of the sales skills.

There are no perfect salespeople. However, Dr. Craft discovered that there are combinations of personality traits that most of the best salespeople possess. In addition to the "Compatibility Charts", the CPQ offers coaching reports that let sales team leaders know what they need to do to coach salespeople and get them quickly ramped up to high productivity.

Before we get too deeply into the technical subject of how personality traits and character traits work together, I need to take care of some credits and disclaimers. All of the information in this book related to the Craft Personality Questionnaire (CPQ®) comes from the *Craft Personality Questionnaire Interpretation Guide,* a "Score Interpretation Guide" (1) published by Previsor, now owned by SHL and the reports generated from the CPQ®. I will also quote from <u>The Basic Eight Traits A Practitioner's Guide to the Administration and Interpretation of the Craft Personality Questionnaire.</u> (2)

"It should be noted that the CPQ measures potential compatibility factors, not necessarily an individual's specific likelihood for success in a particular situation. An individual can be quite successful but unhappy or distressed by an incompatible job description or workplace culture. When selecting personnel, it is recommended that the CPQ be used only in conjunction with other job-related, reliable, and validated selection procedures. Any hiring decision should be based upon a careful review of information derived from thorough competency testing (based on the results of a job analysis) and structured interviews. The best hiring decisions are made when personality assessment is not a stand-alone procedure." (1, p.5)

Over 300,000 individuals were assessed at various stages of the CPQ's development cycles, providing sufficient data to ensure that the assessment is fair, valid, and job-related for use in employment testing. I am advised, to date, that over three million people have been assessed with the CPQ.

Before we study the details of each trait, here is some important information needed to clarify some of the CPQ lingo.

"The CPQ measures eight primary (independent) Personality Traits, as well as numerous secondary (combination) traits that are described in the available reports. These traits have been repeatedly validated as predictors of employee performance in dozens of professions. Where Traits are described, the following general categories apply:

- Low scores are those between 0% and 40%.

- Moderate scores are those between 41% and 60%.

- High scores are those between 61% and 100%.

Trait scores are not to be interpreted in a manner that would suggest that higher scores are always preferred over lower scores, or that lower scores are always of lesser desirability. The terms 'lower' and 'higher' in this context simply refer to the relative position of the participants' trait scores in comparison with the overall distribution of scores in the adult working population (compared to a 50% score on any trait). The specific preference for any given trait (whether lower or higher scores are preferred), referred to as the 'ideal range', is determined by the applicable CPQ model. For example, a lower Detail-orientation is preferred among Account Executives, thus the ideal range for this trait would indicate that higher trait scores are not desirable. An accounting position, in contrast, would require higher Detail-orientation scores." (2, pp.11-12)

Another feature of the CPQ is the "Accuracy/Validity Index". Dr. Craft pioneered this method of catching those candidates who try to fake a personality assessment. For those candidates who work hard to answer the questions in the most favorable way, the CPQ has built-in trip wires that will catch them trying to fake their answers. The scores on this index are "Invalid", "Moderate" and "High". "Invalid" indicates the candidates did not answer the questions in a consistent manner; therefore, the scores cannot be considered an accurate measure of their personality. At this point, you must rely totally on the interview questions to help measure personality traits. "Moderate" indicates some of the wires were tripped, and you must use the scores with caution. "High" scores indicate trustworthy information from the CPQ.

I have helped hundreds of managers interpret thousands of CPQ reports while measuring candidates' over-all fit for a career in sales. In the following chapters, I have done my best to accurately explain the Basic Eight Traits of the CPQ and how they work with each other in combination. My explanation of predicting sales performance by using the Basic Eight Traits in conjunction with the other three elements in the "Best Salesperson Profile" comes from my own personal study and experience. I have spent twenty-eight years studying human behavior, selling products and services, managing salespeople, recruiting salespeople and training sales leaders in these disciplines.

It is recommended that questions regarding the use or interpretation of the CPQ should be directed to someone who is trained in its interpretation and use. I am passionate about using my eleven years of experience in the use of, and interpretation of, the CPQ to assist others in their recruiting efforts.

Chapter 11:

Key Personality Traits

Remember, personality is genetic. It takes less energy to do a task if people have the natural personality tendencies that are in line with particular job duties. It drains their energy if tasks are outside their natural personality tendencies. Personality also determines how people react to their environment. Some people have natural tendencies that help them bounce back more quickly from challenging circumstances.

Listed below is a description of the "Basic Eight" personality traits in the CPQ. After each explanation of the individual traits, I will give a preferred low, moderate or high score range. These general ranges are based upon several CPQ profiles generated by CraftSystems for a variety of sales positions, including both high-activity sales positions (1-30 days in the sales cycle) and strategic sales positions (30+ days in the sales cycle). When you order a CPQ at www.CraftProfiles.com, these various profiles are available to you.

The first four traits are the *ego drive* traits. We are particularly concerned about these four traits since they are responsible for measuring that entrepreneurial, high-spirited, "create something from nothing" salesperson we seek.

They are:

Social Drive

> *"This trait measures individuals' Social Drive or desire for acknowledgement. Through the Social Drive trait, the CPQ helps managers to understand whether individuals are motivated by external and publicized rewards or by private and more personal forms of recognition."(2, p.2)*

Candidates who score in the low range are motivated by personal and private needs, often prefer to work alone and would rather compete against themselves than compete against others. Higher scoring individuals are motivated by a need to be noticed by others. They thrive on situations that reward them with public recognition, prestige, or status. They are often uncomfortable when forced to work alone for extended periods of time.

For organizations where recognition by plaques and awards are part of the culture, high scores on the Social Drive trait are important. When salespeople must go out into the community and network to find prospects, high scores on the Social Drive trait are preferred. Scores on the Social Drive trait help answer these questions about candidates: Will the candidates thrive in an environment where public recognition and awards are part of management's way of rewarding and motivating? Will candidates join networking groups for leads and build rapport with existing clients in order to find enough prospects?

Social Confidence

> *"This trait measures individuals' confidence to take social initiatives and to be assertive when necessary. Through the Social Confidence trait, the CPQ helps managers to identify whether individuals will confidently assert themselves*

or remain timid when dealing with coworkers, customers, and others."(2, p.2)

Lower scoring individuals are uncomfortable when it comes to communicating with strangers or large groups of people. They find it difficult to confidently assert themselves unless they are in safe and familiar situations. Higher scoring individuals assert themselves frequently in routine situations and find it easy to confidently communicate with groups or individuals.

Scores on the Social Confidence trait help answer these questions about candidates: How confident will the candidates be throughout all stages of the sales process? Will they ask for the appointment on the phone, ask for sensitive information in the fact-finding interview, ask for the sale and confidently handle prospects' fears and concerns about the product? Does this candidate have enough social confidence to survive in a high-rejection sales position? Will they have "call reluctance"? High scores on the Social Confidence trait are preferred.

People can have a poor self-image, but still have high scores on the Social Confidence trait. These are the negative people who will tell you what they think (or where you can go) no matter what. Their negativity may be a reflection of their poor self-image and their low Concern for Others, but the fact that they are consistently willing to speak up, no matter what, is reflective of their high scores on the Social Confidence trait. You want to recruit the candidate with high scores on the Social Confidence trait along with high self-image, and the character trait of Concern for Others.

Social Confidence is sometimes confused with hard work ethic. People with low scores on the Social Confidence trait can become immobilized when working on a task where a great deal of Social confidence is required. They quit the task that requires high Social Confidence and go work on a task with no exposure to rejection. I have seen salespeople leave the office and go home after a morning of high-rejection on the phone and do five hours of laborious work in their yard. They ran from the rejection, where they needed high Social Confidence, and ran toward a task where high scores on the Social Confidence trait were not required. They had the Character trait of Work Ethic, but not the Personality trait of high Social Confidence.

Goal-orientation

"This trait measures an individual's goal-oriented drive and intensity level. Using the Goal-orientation trait, the CPQ helps managers to determine whether an individual primarily focuses on efforts in pursuit of identifiable goals or on proceeding through incremental steps in well-defined processes."(2, p.2)

Lower scoring candidates are more even-paced and easy-going, appreciate step-by-step processes and routines and are more methodical. Higher scoring individuals display a natural sense of urgency, prefer results over methods, and focus on the results. They are more concerned with the deadline than the process used to complete the task.

Scores on the Goal-orientation trait help answer questions such as: Do the candidates show a restless and intense drive to hit sales targets in a given time frame? Will they get off to a fast start in a new sales position? Are they a good fit for a fast-paced, high-activity sales environment? If they are in a strategic sales environment, will they exercise patience in working a sales strategy?

When looking at the scores on the Goal-orientation trait, it is important to recognize that this trait does not pertain to peoples' willingness to set goals. It measures how people approach work in relationship to their goals, not whether goals are set.

Some people approach work with more focus on the systems and processes they will use to complete a task and less focus on when they will complete the task. Their goal is, "Do this task correctly without making mistakes". The goal is not necessarily finishing inside a deadline, but on following a process which will aid in doing the task correctly. These people are far more process oriented than deadline oriented, so they will score low on the Goal-orientation trait, and will most likely need to be managed with deadlines. When it comes to sales, salespeople with low Goal-orientation may not have enough sales activities because they are focused too much on the PROCESS rather than the results.

People who score high on the Goal-orientation trait have the goal of, "Do this task quickly to get to the end result". They have a sense of urgency and focus on outcomes. We look for high scores on the Goal-orientation trait because these salespeople want to know how to reach the goals quickly. You also want high Work Ethic so they will stick with the job when it gets hard or boring and not go looking for the faster, easier buck. The best salespeople have learned the discipline of delayed gratification. They have also learned not to get involved in distracting activities or extra "ways to make money" on the side.

High activity selling and strategic selling both require high scores on the Goal-orientation trait. Salespeople who must be more strategic, and who must build multiple relationships during the sales process need to exercise more patience. Salespeople with only moderately high scores on the Goal Orientation trait find it easier to exercise patience during the longer sales cycle than those salespeople with the higher scores.

Some sales managers try to challenge my recommendations, especially in the area of high scores versus low scores on the Goal-orientation trait. Some of them have used the CPQ on a small sampling of their top salespeople, and one of their top performers has low Goal-orientation. Looking at 10,000 salespeople instead of 10 helped us arrive at this recommendation of high scores on the Goal-orientation trait. A larger sample always helps identify the predominant ideal traits. Over time, however, there is always an anomaly.

For instance, there are plow horses and racehorses, and they were bred for different tasks. Every once in a while, you see a farmer who plows with a racehorse instead of a plow horse. It can happen. Mostly, you will see plow horses plowing. The question is, do you want to find the person *most* likely to be wired for success in your field, or do you want to find the exception? You are taking a chance either way, but you are improving your odds by following the statistics that the experts have created.

Need for Control

> *"This trait measures an individual's need for control and independence. Through the Need for Control trait, the CPQ helps managers to identify whether individuals prefer to make decisions independently (working alone) or through collaboration (as part of a team)."* (2, p.2)

Lower scoring individuals value peace and harmony, would rather defer or yield (than cause a conflict) and are "peacemakers" in situations where there is disagreement or conflict. Higher scoring individuals are motivated by independence and freedom, would rather fight for what they believe in than conform, and prefer to work without close supervision.

Scores on the Need for Control trait help answer questions like: Are candidates a good fit for a sales position that does not have a lot of direct supervision? How hard will they work to control conversations, their time and their situations in order to move the sales process along in a timely manner?

Many times, sales managers tell me they want salespeople who are coachable, and who are team players. In response to this common statement from sales managers, I say, "No, you really don't." When I explain the advantages of recruiting salespeople who are prone to be independent and hard to coach, they agree with me. You really want someone who is a challenge to coach, but who listens. You want the independent, "leave me alone" salespeople who are disciplined enough to take wise advice. The best salespeople challenge managers to sharpen their coaching skills. If you are a manager, everything you are learning in this book will help you become a better coach.

High scores on the Goal-orientation and Need for Control traits provide people with an internal clock that helps them set and reach deadlines. These two combination traits help salespeople perform well in a high-activity environment where doing enough of the right types of sales activities in a short period of time is critical for reaching income goals.

If the term "need for control" brings images to mind about a person who manipulates other people in an effort to keep them under their control, you have experienced a person with a combination of high scores on the Need for Control scale along with a low Concern for Others. These people are adept at the manipulation of people. Think of the parent who tries to manipulate the child by saying, "You do not love me." These are the types who use lots of game playing and are to be avoided.

However, salespeople who have a high Need for Control and high Character traits can use these traits to their benefit. They control the phone conversation to get the appointment. They control the fact-finding interview in order to make good use of the prospects' time, as well as their time. They control the sales presentation in order to get to the point where they ask the prospect to buy. They control the rest of the process right up to the final sale. So it works to their advantage, and they can have enough activity to be highly successful.

Let us now turn our attention to the other four "Basic Eight" traits. These four *empathy* traits have to do with how we gather and process information, the degree to which we trust the intentions of others, how hard we work to leave a favorable impression, and whether we focus more on tasks or people. The traits are Detail-orientation, Skepticism, Need to Impress and Need to Nurture. I have not included these empathy traits in the five dimensions of the "Best Salesperson Profile", but they are important to know about, and they often point to areas that will further enhance either success or coaching opportunities for the candidate. The details of each trait are:

Detail-orientation

> *"This trait measures how individuals receive, interpret, and apply information in making decisions. Using the Detail-orientation trait, the CPQ helps managers to identify whether individuals rely upon detailed analysis, or intuition and experience, in making most decisions."* (2. P.3)

Individuals with low scores on the Detail-orientation trait are more reflective and prefer to look at the "big picture". They prefer to delegate detailed analysis to others and use the whole to describe the parts (the "forest" to describe the "trees"). They prefer job duties that require reliance on experience and intuition in decision-making and are more apt to articulate a vision for planning on a large scale. They typically use insight to perceive the needs of others.

Higher scoring individuals are more analytical and prefer to prepare and analyze information, and they use the parts to describe the whole (the "trees" to describe the "forest"). They prefer job duties that require analysis of complex data and painstaking detail and seek to understand complex/technical subject matter. They prefer to use long-term memory to collect and maintain their grasp of important information.

The scores on the Detail-orientation trait help answer these types of questions: Will the candidates focus on getting the right amount of information during the fact-finder or take too long by over analyzing prospects' needs? Will they know when they are ready to get out and start making sales calls or will they become paralyzed by attempting to learn too much information? During the presentation, will they bore prospects with too much information? If they will be selling a complex product, are they capable of focusing on a large amount of details?

The best salespeople, generally speaking, score low on the Detail-orientation trait, even if they sell a complex product. They are focused on knowing just enough details, and giving the prospect just enough detail for the prospect to make a buying decision.

High detail salespeople do not really determine for themselves how much the prospect needs to know. They just assume they will quit talking about the details when the prospect is ready to buy. Unfortunately, that means they talk too much. The prospect may have been ready to buy earlier, if the salesperson had just quit talking. The high Detail-oriented salespeople may suffer from analysis paralysis, a high need to be understood, and a chronic condition of not having sold enough, due to not creating enough sales activities. These are the engineering types, and are more suited to engineering than sales.

People with high scores on the Detail-orientation trait are more likely to succeed if they also have high scores on the Goal-orientation and Social Confidence traits. The high detail-oriented candidates will nearly always struggle with having enough sales activities. They are typically better suited to be the sales engineer that goes along with the salesperson, rather than being the lead.

Good Impression

"This trait measures the motivation to manage the impression left on others. Through the Good Impression

trait, the CPQ helps managers to identify whether an individual will strive to leave a good impression by exaggerating strengths and downplaying weaknesses, or if they will be open and receptive when coached, criticized, or rejected." (2. P.3)

Most other personality tests do not test for the Good Impression trait. I have found it to be an invaluable trait to measure, and unique to CPQ. Candidates who score lower on the Good Impression trait are frank and candid about their fears, faults, and failures; are open to revealing their shortcomings; and are receptive to coaching and supervision. Those with high scores can be defensive or compliant (depending on other CPQ trait scores). They are resilient in the face of opposition and are motivated to leave the most favorable impression.

The scores on the Good Impression trait help answer these types of questions: How resilient to rejection will the candidates be? How will they react to coaching? Will they be prone to embellishment? How prone will they be to accepting responsibility for their actions?

We want candidates with higher scores on the Good Impression and Social Confidence traits. These two traits create the rejection proof salesperson. However, it is critical that these candidates are Honest and have a high Concern for Others. Without these important character traits, we get a person who is very prone to dishonesty and egotism.

People with low scores on the Good Impression and Social Confidence traits can become immobilized by rejection. They begin to stop putting themselves into situations where they may get rejected. I will not deselect candidates because of a low score on the Good Impression trait if they have a high score on the Social Confidence trait. However, I do want to check and see how they deal with rejection.

It is easy to spot the person with high scores on the Good Impression trait. Be cautious when candidates bring a big notebook with tabs showing all of their accomplishments. Listen carefully to the way they describe their weaknesses. Many times, candidates spin strengths to sound like weaknesses. Examples of these statements are: "I am impatient with lazy people", "I am a workaholic", or "I am frugal". When I interview this type candidate, I immediately begin to measure the Honesty trait.

The combination of low scores on the Skepticism trait and high scores on the Good Impression trait is a big "red flag". I have experienced many times when candidates with these combination scores *believe* the embellishments they are telling me! The CPQ does not measure Honesty; however, my experience tells me to spend a lot of time measuring the Honesty trait when I see this combination of personality traits.

I interviewed a man once who said that he was laid off from his last sales job because they followed a "last in, first out" policy in making their cuts. I challenged him, and told him that I happened to know his former supervisor, and this story did not sound consistent with his logic. I told him that I knew there was no way the supervisor would let a policy like that stand in the way of keeping a top producing salesperson, as you just told me you were. I asked him, "Does that sound confusing to you?"

He said. "Yes, I didn't understand his reasoning either, but that is what he told me." He believed his own embellishment.

I have found that people who score really high on the Good Impression trait always have a "good answer" for every question. Sometimes it is hard to get to the truth. If you are interested in candidates with these high scores (95-100%), spend a LOT of time with them, and be SURE you check their references. Review the section on checking references.

Also, make sure you are asking for and getting specific examples of what candidates tell you. Candidates with high scores on the Good Impression trait are very good at speaking in convincing but vague generalities. Ask, "Will you please give me an example of that?" If a specific example cannot be given, they simply have a philosophy about a situation that did not actually occur.

As I mentioned earlier, people who are resilient to rejection may not be very coachable. Just because you think salespeople with high scores on the Good Impression trait are not coachable, do not give up on them, but do not expect their agreement when they are sitting in front of you. Give them your advice and move on. They may or may not listen. They may think about it later and agree, although they will most likely not give you credit for it. You should realize successful salespeople will likely consider your advice later.

High scores on the Good Impression trait will show up on a resume with superlative words like best ever, perfect, undeniable, do not care what people think, and an overuse of the word "I." People with high scores will consistently follow up your story with one of their own that is better. Just make sure this "one up on you" behavior is not annoying. Those with low scores on the Good Impression trait will use words like straight shooter, transparent, forgiving, readily admits faults and failures, etc.

Need to Nurture

> *"This trait measures individuals' desire to nurture and care for others. Through the Need to Nurture trait, the CPQ helps managers to understand whether individuals are motivated by opportunities to help and serve others, or to remain formal and "on task".* (2. P.3)

Candidates who score low on the Need to Nurture trait are more task-oriented than service-oriented. They typically avoid sharing their intimate feelings with others. They manage their time and efforts efficiently and demonstrate "on task" behavior more readily than others. Higher scoring individuals are warm and sensitive to the needs of others and enjoy sharing intimate feelings with others. They prefer job duties that allow them to serve others and nurture long-term relationships and are more concerned with others' feelings than efficiency.

The scores on the Need to Nurture trait help answer these questions about candidates: Are they prone to being good listeners while discovering the needs of prospects and while making the presentation? How will they manage time and resources in accomplishing daily tasks? Will they prioritize their work in support of business goals? How driven are these individuals to focus on the needs of other people during the sales process?

Low scores on the Need to Nurture trait represent the ideal range for both successful salespeople and sales team leaders. If you are spending too much time helping people who will never buy your product, you are too concerned about the wrong people. I like to see a score on the Need to Nurture trait in the 30-40% range. Candidates with these scores also need the character trait of a high Concern for Others.

You want someone whose basic attitude is, "Yes, I am task oriented, but I want to do the right thing. Yes, I am task oriented, but I want to take care of my customers. Yes, I am task oriented, but I care about my daughter and she needs me to listen to her while she cries when she is upset." People with high scores on the Need to Nurture trait are naturally good listeners. Low scorers need to learn to ask good open-ended questions and not talk too much.

Watch out for the combination of low scores on the Goal-orientation trait and high scores on the Need to Nurture trait. These candidates are process oriented and people oriented, and do not have an internal clock that says get on with it, move on. Fact-finding and presentations drag on much too long. They are too concerned with making people feel good.

It is easy to like candidates who have high scores on the Need to Nurture trait. People with high scores on the Need to Nurture, Good Impression and Social Drive traits are really good at getting you to like them. I have seen dozens of salespeople that everyone likes, but they are failing at sales because they do not have enough activity. The number one tragedy in building a sales team is hiring the people everyone likes, but who are failing at sales. Their closing ratio is often double that of the other sales reps, but they do not make enough sales presentations. It is not about being liked. It is about having enough activity and being liked.

When I finally started ignoring people who had "sparkle," I became a better recruiter. Looking at "sparkle" blinds you to the real reasons you should hire or should not hire someone.

Skepticism

"This trait measures individuals' Skepticism and trust of fellow employees, managers, and others. Through the Skepticism trait, the CPQ helps managers to identify whether individuals are open and trusting, or guarded and skeptical, in workplace interactions." (2. P.3)

This trait is not genetic but is influenced mostly by how people have been treated in work related environments; therefore, scores on this trait may or may not fluctuate based on recent experiences. The candidates who score low on the Skepticism trait are trusting of the intentions of others and give others the benefit of the doubt until proven wrong. They accept what management says without challenge. Higher scoring individuals are more cautious, formal and rigid and distrust the intentions of others until these individuals "prove themselves". They are guarded in their enthusiasm for new ideas.

The scores on the Skepticism trait help answer these questions about candidates: Are they optimistic about impacting their future? Will the candidates be able to determine which leads are viable? How quickly will they trust the intentions of you as their manager and co-workers? Are they naive?

The ideal score on the Skepticism trait is high. Salespeople do not need to believe everything a prospect tells them. If the prospect says, "Oh yes, I love your proposal, and I'll call you tomorrow." Highly skeptical salespeople do not believe this smoke screen, but work to uncover hidden reasons why the prospect is not making an immediate buying decision. Salespeople also should not be so skeptical that they dismiss prospects too early, or become dysfunctional in their distrust of co-workers for no reason. If their Skepticism is too high, they read too much negativity into every situation. A good balance of discernment is important.

> After we hire someone through the use of the "Recruit the Best" system, we know, with a great deal of certainty, which specific sales skills will require the greatest amount of coaching.

People with low scores on the Skepticism trait are very trusting. When I see a low score, I begin to look for signs of naïveté. They may or may not be naive. Remember, this personality trait is not genetic but environmental. People who grew up in a low-crime town, and/or whose upbringing included loving parents with few bad work experiences, may have good reason not to be skeptical. One likely scenario of salespeople with a strong cultural foundation is that they will probably have an easier time getting through a crisis when life gets hard than those without such a foundation.

When I see a low Skepticism score from candidates who do not describe an ideal upbringing; or they have had multiple negative job experiences; or a bad family situation; or a divorce where their trust was violated; yet they still have a low Skepticism score, I tend to believe they are not facing reality. They do not seem to live in the real world. Proceed with extreme caution. *(I do not ask questions to get candidates to reveal this type of personal information. People with low scores on the Skepticism trait have a tendency to reveal a lot of this information unsolicited.)*

Since the Skepticism trait is environmentally based, you might find that candidates who have recently left a bad situation tend to have an abnormally high Skepticism score. It is important to know the difference between chronic Skepticism and situational Skepticism. We discover the difference with good interview questions.

Candidates with low Work Ethic and low Skepticism are likely to be naïve and exercise poor judgment. The Candidates with high Work Ethic, high Concern for Others and high Skepticism provide a voice of reason when scrutinizing details. They are discerning of prospects' intentions to buy, and they use good sales skills to get prospects to buy in a timely manner. However, people with high Skepticism may make sarcastic or biased statements about others during the interview process, and may question your intentions or the things you tell them.

Now that we have the foundation of each of the "Basic Eight" traits in the CPQ, it is important to build on this knowledge base. Let us begin with a quick review. There are five dimensions of the "Best Salesperson Profile". We screen for the right Attitudes and Motivations. When candidates pass the test for these two dimensions, we measure Character traits by looking at the past influence of parents and mentors. After we determine that candidates have the necessary Character traits, we use science (CPQ) to measure for the right combination of personality traits for performing sales tasks in a high-activity, high-rejection environment.

Two Important Areas of Human Behavior

As we continue to peal back the layers of the candidates' past in order to predict their future performance, it is necessary to get more technical and learn more details in these two important areas of human behavior and the "Recruit the Best" system:

1. The first important area of human behavior focuses on this fact: *Behavior can be predicted based upon the way the "Basic Eight" personality traits work in combination with each other.* For example, some people who score high on the Social Confidence trait may come across as intimidating and unconcerned. Other people who score high on the Social Confidence trait may come across as warm and concerned about their needs. Whether they appear to be intimidating or warm depends upon their scores on the Need to Nurture trait. Once we learn these important combination personality traits, we can begin to more accurately measure candidates' potential to master the sales skills. After we hire someone through the use of the "Recruit the Best" system, we know, with a great deal of certainty, which specific sales skills will require the greatest amount of coaching.

2. The second important area of human behavior focuses on this fact: *The high and low scores on each of the eight personality traits point to which of the four character traits will cause us the greatest struggles.* Once we know the candidates' possible character challenges, we can better measure these character traits with targeted interview questions.

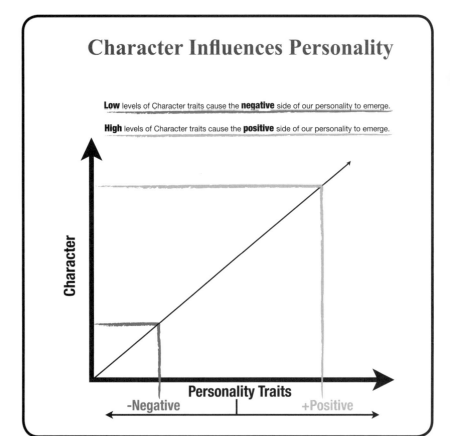

Keep in mind that all personality traits have a good side and a dark side. The same trait that helps us confidently ask prospects to buy our product can also have the dark side of running over others or intimidating others to get what we want. Character helps us choose the good side of our personality traits.

Once you learn these personality and character combinations, your knowledge of human behavior grows to a very high level, and the interviewing and selection process becomes much easier. You begin to make better recruiting decisions and retain more new salespeople. As I work with managers on a weekly basis, they tell me that learning about these combination Character and Personality traits is the most valuable area of the "Recruit the Best" system.

We all agree that people are complicated, and the lack of understanding of human complexity is the main reason that making recruiting decisions is so difficult. In the remaining pages, I want to take the above two areas of human behavior and explain each in a way that will give you a knowledge base that you will need to effectively use the tools in the "Recruit the Best" system. It is a combination of this knowledge base and the recruiting tools that will fill the gap in your recruiting efforts.

Chapter 12:

Measuring Character and Personality Combinations

Let us begin with the first fact discussed at the end of the last chapter. ***Behavior can be predicted based upon the way the "Basic Eight" personality traits work in combination with each other.*** The CPQ creates a "Compatibility Chart". This chart shows the ideal scores for the "Basic Eight" traits for a specific occupation. When you use the CPQ at my Website, you can choose from several different "baseline" compatibility profiles that have been created by Dr. Craft. The "Compatibility Chart" will show your candidates' actual scores compared to the ideal scores for the profile against which you choose to measure them. You simply choose the "baseline" profile that best fits the salesperson who can sell in your industry. If you desire, we can get more specific and build a custom profile for your company. I am available to assist you with this step of using the CPQ.

For the sake of our discussion, I will be referring to the scores on the "Basic Eight" traits by using the scores found on one of the profiles for a salesperson working in the following sales environment:

- Prospecting and networking to find leads is required.

- Salespeople must phone/email/cold call to set first appointments.

- The first appointment is an introduction appointment that should result in a fact-finding effort to diagnose needs of the prospect. The presentation follow-up meeting is set at the end of this first meeting. There may be a need for additional fact-finding meetings with other decision makers.

- At the second meeting, the presentation is made to all decision makers and addresses the specific needs of the prospect. Fears, concerns and objections are handled in a way that the salesperson gets the sale.

- Salespeople use the resulting relationship to get referrals to other prospects.

Your sales environment may not be exactly like this, but it will be easy for you to translate the application to your specific situation. Custom information can be created for any company. A specific, validated profile can be created for your sales team.

A Validated Benchmark Profile

When recruiting salespeople for a sales team in the environment described above, the validated benchmark profile provided below will help many sales managers use the CPQ inside the "Recruit the Best" system. This profile was validated using four large companies in the same industry, two hundred sixty-five sales offices, and ten thousand salespeople. The ideal scores on this profile for the "Basic Eight" traits are as follows:

Social Drive   90-100%

0   50   100

Social Confidence   45-75%

0   50   100

Goal-orientation   90-100%

0   50   100

Need for Control   50-75%

0   50   100

Detail-orientation   10-35%

0   50   100

Skepticism   50-80%

0   50   100

Good Impression   60-90%

0   50   100

Need to Nurture   15-40%

0   50   100

These CPQ scores are indicative of salespeople who have the drive and confidence to perform at a high level in a high-activity, high-rejection and competitive environment where it is necessary to create "something from nothing". They have an independent, entrepreneurial spirit that can work with low amounts of supervision.

Remember, the CPQ gives us the information we need in the Personality traits dimension, which is only one of the five dimensions of the "Best Salesperson Profile". Even when we find candidates who score in all the ideal ranges, it does not mean they have high levels of all the other four dimensions. We must complete all the steps in the process and score the candidates in all five areas of the "Best Salesperson Profile" using the "Matching Score Sheet".

Now that you have a recruiting system, and understand how to measure Attitudes, Motivations and Character traits, you will find that there will be many times when candidates have high scores in these three areas, but will have some scores on the CPQ that are not near the ideal ranges. This is the time in the recruiting process when it becomes necessary to understand how *"behavior can be predicted based upon the way certain personality traits work in combination."* It is important to learn which combination traits may be low-risk combinations and which may be high-risk combinations.

Before we look at specific combinations, let us fold the second fact of human behavior into our formula. ***The high and low scores on each of the eight personality traits point to which of the four character traits will cause us the greatest struggles.*** We cannot change our personality. We can only manage how our personality traits manifest themselves in daily relationships with others. We work on and acquire strong character traits and use them to control the negative side of our personality traits. During the interview process, we want to use interview questions to measure whether or not candidates have acquired the best character traits that work in combination with their genetic personality.

While recruiting salespeople in the environment we have just described, I have identified some important personality and character combinations. *I will describe the combination traits, describe the patterns of behavior to which these traits point, and then tell you how to use the tools in the system to determine whether or not candidates have overcome these challenges.* Remember, these combination traits do not guarantee the behaviors, they simply point to potential natural tendencies. The names given to these combination traits are created by me and are not used in the CPQ reports. I have created them to help enhance the training process.

Analysis Paralysis Paul

Social Confidence   95%

| 0 | 50 | 100 |

Goal-orientation   25%

| 0 | 50 | 100 |

Detail-orientation   80%

| 0 | 50 | 100 |

Need to Nurture   25%

| 0 | 50 | 100 |

Low scores on the Goal-orientation trait and high scores on the Detail-orientation trait indicate that Paul will most likely get paralyzed by over-analyzing details. Paul thinks he needs to know all the details of the product before he can get out and make sales calls. He has a tendency to give prospects too much information during the sales presentation. His high scores on the Social Confidence trait indicate that he may have the tendency to come across as a "know-it-all". Paul's low scores on the Need to Nurture trait indicate that he may have a tendency to overpower people with his knowledge and make them feel "stupid". Both of these tendencies result in low levels of critical sales activities. He is respected for being really smart and for his product knowledge, but he may not share his knowledge with enough people to hit sales targets.

If you are considering hiring Paul, make sure he has a strong Concern for Others and a very strong Work Ethic. He will need the Concern for Others to soften his high scores on the Social Confidence trait and low scores on the Need to Nurture trait. Even with a strong work ethic, Paul will need enough money saved to make it through months of low sales results, and you will need enough patience and resources to help him through a long "ramp up" period.

Too Much Nurturing Nancy

Social Drive   60%

0   50   100

Social Confidence   65%

0   50   100

Goal-orientation   25%

0   50   100

Need to Nurture   80%

0   50   100

This personality trait combination is the first cousin to "Analysis Paralysis Paul". Rather than spending too much time on details, Nancy spends too much time nurturing people during the sale process. Her confident, social, warm, and charming personality causes people to like her quickly. She may even be a good networker and respected in her social circles. She is a good listener, but struggles to have enough weekly sales calls due to spending too much time with people who most likely do not have the resources to afford the purchase. She may also spend too much time with people who are not going to make a buying decision any time soon. Even with a strong work ethic, you will have the same time-management struggles with Nancy as with Paul in the previous example.

During the interview, Nancy is very charming and charismatic. Her high scores on the Need to Nurture trait and her high scores on the Social Drive trait indicate that she can focus on you with a disarming charm. With this type of candidate, it is very important not to let your emotions take over. Remember to simply ask the interview questions, take notes and move to the next question. Avoid the temptation to mirror Nancy's charming personality back to her. If you are considering hiring either a Paul or Nancy, make sure he or she has a documented history of sales results, in a similar industry to yours, over several years.

Peter the Pleaser

Social Drive   60%

0   50   100
_____●_____

Social Confidence   40%

0   50   100
_____●_____

Goal-orientation   45%

0   50   100
_____●_____

Need for Control   20%

0   50   100
_____●_____

Good Impression   90%

0   50   100
_____●____

Peter's high scores on the Good Impression trait indicate that he may have a tendency to exaggerate his strengths and downplay his weaknesses. People with high scores on the Good Impression trait are either pleasers or egotists. Peter is a pleaser, which is indicated by his low scores on the Social Confidence and Need for Control traits. He has a tendency to work hard to tell you what he thinks you want to hear because he is pleasing, submissive, compliant and loyal. You may initially think these descriptions of Peter sound like good traits. Remember, Peter needs to perform sales tasks in a high-activity, high-rejection environment. These traits also cause him to be sensitive to rejection. He will avoid sales activities that consistently put him in stressful sales situations. He is the salesperson who avoids asking the tough questions during the interview because he is afraid he might offend the prospect. His presentations are full of details, but he never gets around to asking people to buy. His favorite phrase is, "I just don't want to come across as pushy."

Just like Nancy in the previous example, Peter will be charming during the interview. He will be working hard to impress you throughout the interview. Peter may score high in all four of the character traits. He may believe in the product and have great passion for selling. He can be very motivated to make money as a salesperson. This does not mean he can sell, especially with this "pleaser" personality. Be sure to ask for written records that back up Peter's claims of high sales performance. Ask references if you can depend on what Peter tells you.

I have seen many salespeople like Peter, who have high scores on the Social Drive trait, but low scores on the Social Confidence trait struggle in networking groups. He is driven to attend networking groups because of the need for social interaction, but he does not have the confidence to network while he is at the meetings. He drops out and finds many reasons why "networking meetings just didn't work" for him. He will then not rise to the challenge of finding a steady flow of new referrals to call.

Eddie the Embellishing Egotist or Tom the Trusted Charismatic

Social Confidence 90%

0   50   100

Goal-orientation 75%

0   50   100

Need for Control 90%

0   50   100

Good Impression   100%

0	50	100

Accuracy/Validity Index - *Moderate*

Let us assume that we have two candidates, Eddie and Tom, who have the exact same scores on the personality traits listed above. However, when you meet them, they portray two different personalities. Tom is a very trusted and charismatic top performing salesperson. Eddie is also a top performing salesperson, but struggles with honesty and humility.

The difference between Tom and Eddie is that Tom has worked hard to acquire the character traits of Concern for Others and Honesty. These two character traits help Tom remain humble and suppress any desires to embellish the truth to get what the wants. He realizes the same personality traits that help him confidently control the sales process also have a dark side that could cause him to be intimidating and impatient with others.

Eddie, on the other hand, does not have sufficient motivation to realize that the same traits that help him confidently present his products in a very compelling and convincing manner also cause him to struggle with honesty and humility. He chooses to feed his own selfish desires by manipulating others.

The tools in the "Recruit the Best" system will help you discern the Toms from the Eddies. The reference check is critical. When I hear things like, "That Eddie is a real handful", it becomes easy to match this comment to the CPQ chart. The reference source just told me, in a joking way, that Eddie is an egotist. Candidates with these personality trait combinations really struggle with admitting their faults and taking personal responsibility for their mistakes.

In addition to focusing on the questions that measure Honesty and Concern for Others, make sure you are accurately measuring for the character trait of Responsibility.

Love Her But Can't Sell Laura

Social Drive   89%

0   50   100

Social Confidence   65%

0   50   100

Goal-orientation   25%

0   50   100

Need to Control   25%

0   50   100

Good Impression   30%

0   50   100

Laura is a very outgoing, genuine and an extremely likable person. From her resume, she appears to have the sales experience you desire. During the interview, she passed the screening on Attitudes, Motivations and Character. All her references say great things about her. She has the sales records to back up her claims of success. You hire her. Six months later, it is evident that she will never survive in your industry. What went wrong?

Most likely she was successful in an industry that did not have the same demands as those of your industry. Her references were not necessarily totally pleased with her production levels, but reluctant to criticize anyone as nice as Laura. She is also too nice to fire. She is the "all talk, no action" worker. Companies are full of these types of low producing salespeople. Their high Social Drive and Social Confidence scores mask their low Goal-orientation and low Need for Control scores. They get away with low productivity levels by charming their way through life. The high scores in the Need for Control and Goal-orientation traits provide the internal clock needed in a fast-paced, high-activity sales environment. Those with low scores on these two traits will most likely not move at a fast enough pace to have enough sales activities in a given period of time.

Pat the Independent Entrepreneur

Social Drive   89%

0   50   100

Social Confidence   90%

0   50   100

Goal-orientation   95%

0   50   100

Need to Control   80%

0   50   100

Good Impression   70%

0   50   100

Pat is likely to be a superstar, or superstar in the making. If you have a sales culture where independent, entrepreneurial salespeople thrive, Pat has the combination personality traits you are looking for. Her high Social Drive Scores cause her to love to network and accumulate a lot of relationships for the purpose of doing business. The high scores in Social Confidence, Goal-orientation, Need for Control and Good Impression traits indicate a combination of a driven, confident and independent minded entrepreneur. Pat knows how to say "yes" to the tasks that matter and "no" to those that do not matter. She is the type of person who would load up her covered wagon and leave the original thirteen colonies to go fight the elements just for the excitement of the challenge.

Just as this personality has potential for being a successful entrepreneurial salesperson, there is equally potential for a disastrous career. Anytime people have strong personality traits, they need equally strong character traits to make sure the good side and not the dark side of these combination traits come out. The same confidence and drive that help Pat convince others to buy, must be dovetailed with a Work Ethic so that she does not get too impatient for results and start moving too quickly to the next perceived opportunity.

In my work, I have seen people with Pat's combination of personality traits and strong character traits of Work Ethic and Responsibility become successful in everything they attempt. I have also seen people with these personality traits jump form one idea to the next and never accomplish anything of significance due to their lack of focus brought about by a low Work Ethic. You must measure Character and Personality in combination! The reason there are so few entrepreneurs that make it is that there are few with the Work Ethic to go along with their high scores on the Social Confidence and Goal-orientation traits.

Clay the Clydesdale

Social Drive   35%

0   50   100

Social Confidence   80%

0   50   100

Goal-orientation   40%

0   50   100

Need to Control   35%

0   50   100

Clay is the salesperson who ramps up quickly, but this is because he comes in early and stays late. He has an extremely high Work Ethic that causes him to work long hours to do whatever it takes to get the job done. His high score on the Social Confidence trait is an asset at all steps of the sales process. His low score on the Goal-orientation trait indicates that he does not work with the same fast-step and fire-in-the-belly as the entrepreneur. Although he has the same amount of sales activities, it takes more hours in the day for him to reach his goals. I have seen many of these Clydesdale types. They often have a harder time balancing family and work because it takes so many hours for them to reach their sales targets. It is important for Clay to have good administrative help.

Fran the Family Diehard

Social Drive   45%

0   50   100

Social Confidence	55%		
0	50		100

Goal-orientation	45%		
0	50		100

Need to Control	40%		
0	50		100

Fran has a family to support. Because of a strong sense of Responsibility, hard Work Ethic and Concern for others, Fran pushes her energy up every day to perform at the level indicated by the higher scores of these personality traits. When scores on the CPQ are in the moderate range, the candidates' circumstances and other factors will determine whether they operate on the high side or the low side of the trait without the extreme behaviors of the trait. Because of the high Motivation of the need to support her family, Fran pushes her energy up to the high side. Fran's years of sales experience are also contributing factors of success.

I have a word of caution about Fran's combination of traits. If you are recruiting salespeople without experience, this combination of traits is somewhat risky. After you have determined the candidates have the right Attitudes, it is critical to make sure they have sufficient financial motivation to push their energy up when they hit the "sweat zone". Without sufficient financial needs, the chances are slim that people with this profile will hit sales targets.

If you recruit candidates with Fran's combination of personality traits who have the Attitudes and Character traits, and you have the time and resources to invest in them, there is a chance they will evolve to a point of consistent quota production. Notice

I said, "Quota production", not "Above quota production." If they make it, they will most likely be a steady producer who never rises to greatness. They finally make it by developing a strong enough clientele to now sustain them. Do not use this as a model for building your sales team. People with Fran's traits are very slow starters, but can become solid members of the team if you have the time and patience to develop them, and if they can hang on financially through months or even years of low commissions.

Children can be the best evidence of "hard-wired" personality traits.

The "Basic Eight" traits in the CPQ have never been more visible for me than in my own two children. When they were teenagers, we all decided to build a lodge on our farm in the Great Smoky Mountains. For 18 months, we drove an hour every weekend to get to the job site. That represented a lot of weekends and a lot of work, especially for teenagers.

Each time we would load up the car for the trek to the farm, my daughter would fidget restlessly in her seat. She would quiz me about my expectations for the day and the tasks specifically assigned to her. My son took advantage of the long drive to be able to sleep.

When we arrived, my daughter jumped quickly from the vehicle to begin her tasks, just as we had talked about on the way. It was important for me to check on her regularly. She was prone to working too quickly, and being more focused on completion than on doing it right. She and I both quickly worked up a sweat as we began the tasks of the day.

My son and wife, on the other hand, worked into the day more slowly. One day, I noticed that they each strolled into the unfinished building with empty buckets they had picked up on the site. My curiosity got the best of me as I watched to see what they were going to do with their respective buckets. They turned them upside down and sat on them, as they both looked around admiring the scenery. I looked directly at my son, and he responded with his big smile. "Dad, I love coming here and working with you and the family. I just love the smell of cut wood early in the morning. What would you like for me to do?"

Firmly biting my tongue to keep from showing my impatience, I took him into a room and gave him specific instructions about using the miter saw to put boards on the unfinished walls. He began working very hard like a Clydesdale: slow, steady and methodical, and making very few mistakes. Soon, I noticed that the noise from the saw had stopped. When I went to investigate, I found him back on his bucket seat, admiring the work he had done on one of the walls. He again thanked me for letting him come to work with me, and asked if I liked what he had done. In fact, the wall he worked on was skillfully finished.

"But son," I asked as non-judgmentally as I could, "why did you not finish the other three walls?" "You didn't tell me," he replied, quite innocently.

My daughter, on the other hand, was always trying to rush ahead, deciding on her own what she wanted to do, then trying to get it finished. I had to manage her differently because she was prone to rushing and taking short cuts. Sometimes she was satisfied with finishing, rather than finishing well. She was also prone to quitting one task and starting another because she became easily bored with repetitive work.

This scenario played out many times as we worked to finish the lodge. Although my son and daughter both completed the same amount of work each day, they needed to be managed in very different ways. My son needed to be told which task to work on next. He worked more slowly and methodically, and took a bit longer to do a task, but it was always good work. He did not want to begin another task for fear of doing something I did not want him to do.

Both of my children possess a genetically hard-wired personality that caused one to approach work patiently and methodically, and the other to approach it at a fast, restless pace. They both needed to be taught hard Work Ethic. My daughter needed Work Ethic to slow down and stay on task even though she was bored. My son needed Work Ethic to get him started on a task and to avoid sitting around too much on his bucket while waiting to be told what to do.

Having had the personality assessment training prior to this experience was a godsend. Otherwise, I would have most likely been building the lodge alone after having run off all my help with my naturally impatient management style. I, too, had to adjust in order to provide the leadership that was needed for the team to function well. My son was like the hard working Clydesdale, but needed the periodic nudge to keep moving. He needed specific instructions on what to do and how to do it, and he prefers close supervision until he is completely sure of what he is doing. My daughter needed supervision on doing the job right, and staying focused on a single task until it was completed.

Today, both children have followed this same genetically programmed pace of work. My son is a golf instructor who methodically analyzes golfers' swings, and patiently teaches them correct techniques to hit the golf ball well. My daughter is an entrepreneurial business owner who is self-motivated, enjoys working long hours, and continues the restless pace of work I first observed when we were building our lodge together. My son will readily admit that he works better with structure and rules. My daughter thrives on independence and flexibility. We are born with our hard-wired genetics, but our home life and culture shape our character traits.

Chapter 13:

Tips for Screening Resumes

With the hope of assisting you along this path, I have provided notes on screening resumes that continue to assist me as I recruit and train others to recruit. I have read many studies that say you only get 2% of the information you need from a resume to make a good hiring decision. I tend to agree with this conclusion. However, I have discovered some ways to use the information about human behavior that you have learned from this book to look for the five dimensions of the "Best Salesperson Profile" in the resume.

One word of caution: The more help candidates receive when writing their resumes, the more difficult it will be to measure the elements in the "Best Salesperson Profile" by looking at the resumes. Most resume services and their writers are not really skilled enough to write the information the sales manager wants to hear. Instead, they map their own biography onto the candidates' resumes. Words have

> After spending more time with candidates in whom I have a strong interest, I continue to look at the resume for subtle clues that reveal character and personality traits.

power, nonetheless. So listen carefully to the candidates' choices of words in the interview, as well as on their resume and other written communications.

After spending more time with candidates in whom I have a strong interest, I continue to look at the resume for subtle clues that reveal character and personality traits. I continue to be amazed at the things I discover. Recently, during the final interview, I discovered that the candidate did not actually finish school and obtain the degree that was indicated on the resume. After this discovery, I began to see a pattern of embellishments on the resume. This pattern highlighted a key character flaw that was not as evident during the other stages of the recruiting process. For me, the resume is not only used at the beginning during the screening step, but throughout the entire selection process.

The following are some important tips to use when screening resumes and when referring to the resume throughout the recruiting process:

Evidence of negative attitude toward sales as a career:

- A lack of consistent history of sales awards. Winning one or two monthly sales contests during a twelve-month period, and not remaining in the top-performing group throughout the rest of the year points to a sporadic performance.

- A history of being in sales for a period of time, switching to operations or management, then back into sales points toward a negative image as a salesperson.

- Selling products in a low-activity, low-stress environment. Some retail, customer service, and account management positions are in this category.

Evidence of motivation to meet immediate needs and make the future better:

- Changes in jobs that have resulted in advancement and income growth

- "Objective" at beginning of resume is specific toward sales and uses growth words like, "advancement, opportunity, and growth".

Evidence of Honesty/Dishonesty:

- Overstating accomplishments:

    - Lists accomplishments of team/club/organization of which they were a part. *(Truth – their role was minimal. Did the least amount of work to get the activity listed on resume.)*

    - Won monthly sales award 1-2 times in a 12-24 month period – *(Truth – sandbagged to win a monthly award.)*

    - Rounding up on GPA – 3.0 *(Truth – 2.7)*

    - Exaggerating job responsibilities – "coached salespeople" *(Truth – ran the sales meetings a few times when the manager was out of town.)*

Evidence of Concern for Others:

- Contributed in a significant way to accomplish something for others:

    - Community service – raised money, volunteered at mission, taught class at religious organizations, worked for Habitat for Humanity, etc.

    - Member of community service organization – Rotary, Kiwanis, Lions, Optimist, Civitan, etc.

Evidence of Hard Work Ethic:

- Working at the same company/career for an extended period of time
- Reasons for changing companies related to movement up
- Awards for achievement in sports, academics, and sales
- Use of words like "hard work, discipline, achievement, and putting in long hours"
- Worked to pay for education

Evidence of showing Personal Responsibility for Decisions:

- Gives reasons for leaving job as a movement up
- Does not talk badly about previous bosses/coworkers/companies

Evidences of the Social Drive Trait:

- *High Social Drive:*

    - Uses words like – award winner, competitive, proud
    - Shows interest in plaques and awards
    - Involved in networking groups – Business Networking International (BNI)

- *Low Social Drive:*

    - Strongly focused on educational accomplishments
    - Personal activities involve being alone or with a few people

Evidences of the Social Confidence Trait:

- *High Social Confidence:*
    - Uses words like confident, leader, closer, fearless, assertive
    - Strongly focused on job/career accomplishments
    - Held leadership positions
    - Leader in networking groups
    - Leader in the community
    - Public speaking experience

- *Low Social Confidence:*
    - "Objective" statement - "canned" and not specifically related to sales/service duties.
    - Strongly focused on educational accomplishments

Evidences of the Goal-orientation Trait:

- *High Goal-orientation:*
    - Uses words like – driven, goal oriented, focused, results oriented, intense, likes to learn, likes to grow
    - Strongly focused on job/career accomplishments
    - Held leadership positions
    - Focuses on many awards, accomplishments and rising to the top

- *Low Goal-orientation:*
    - Uses words like – methodical, consistent, collaborative
    - Overall mediocre resume

- Focuses on use of systems and processes
- Several gaps in employment

Evidences of the Need for Control Trait:

- *High Need for Control:*
    - Uses words like – leader, negotiator, versatile, takes charge, strong sales skills, seeks to work as part of small company with less direct supervision
    - Held leadership/management positions on the job and in community activities
    - Involved in entrepreneurial business/activities
- *Low Need for Control:*
    - Uses words like – team oriented, harmony, peacemaker and mediator
    - Held supportive roles rather than management/ leadership roles

Evidences of the Detail Orientation Trait:

- *High Detail Orientation:*
    - Uses words like – analytical, detail oriented, I think, organized, complex problem solver
    - Held jobs that require high detail analysis
- *Low Detail Orientation:*
    - Uses words like – visionary, big picture oriented, feel
    - Typos, misspelled words, poor sentence structure
    - Generic resume/not specific to job with your company

Evidences of the Good Impression Trait:

- *High Good Impression:*

    - Uses words like – the best ever made, number one, undeniable and perfect

    - Over-uses the word "I"

Low Good Impression:

    - Uses words like – straight shooter, forgiving, open to advice

Evidences of the Need to Nurture Trait:

- *High Need to Nurture:*

    - Uses words like – service, good listener, feelings, caring, sensitive, people oriented, warm, relationship focused and share

    - Involved in activities that help people solve personal problems – church related activities, big brother/sister, solves family issues

- *Low Need to Nurture:*

    - Uses words like – I think, on task, efficient, tough negotiator, focused, results oriented

    - Resume full of projects and tasks with fewer people oriented activities

Chapter 14:

Growing From a Good Sales Leader to a Great Sales Leader

Congratulations for taking the time to read this book. I have done my best to provide you a system to assist you in growing from a good sales leader to a great sales leader. It has taken over a quarter of a century of my career in sales, sales management and consulting to acquire the knowledge contained in these pages and to create the "Recruit the Best" system. The creation of this system has been a joint effort of my business partner, Lance Cooper, and myself. Lance is a genius when it comes to developing systems and training programs. It is my hope that you will continue to study and use the tools in the "Recruit the Best" system to build and retain a strong sales team.

By studying the five dimensions in the "Best Salesperson" Profile throughout this book, you have learned the answer to the question, "WHAT do I look for when recruiting salespeople?" By learning about the set of customized tools and the CPQ, you have learned to answer the question, "HOW do I look for these dimensions in candidates?" You now have a guideline to help you know WHERE to go to find the best salespeople candidates. I encourage you to master the entire system, not just casually use bits and pieces of the tools. This mastery requires obtaining the knowledge of human behavior, then dovetailing this knowledge with the tools and processes inside the system.

Many sales leaders say they do not want to be a psychologist; they just want to be good sales leaders. A degree in psychology is not necessary. I do believe, however, that an in-depth understanding of human behavior, along with skills in using the tools inside a "best practice" recruiting system, are necessary to become a *great* sales leader. Knowledge of human behavior is the most important asset of a great sales leader. The more you understand human behavior, the easier your life and job become. We all need this knowledge to make relationships work. This includes marriage and parenting, as well as relationships at work.

Lance Cooper, my business partner, has defined success as, "Doing your best every day for the benefit of others." My encouragement to you is to accept this definition of success into your life and work hard every day to make a difference in the world around you. The most important difference you can make in people's lives is guiding them into an occupation where their natural talents and abilities help them do their best every day for the benefit of others. You have what it takes.

Go do your best for the benefit of others!

Complete Set of Customized Tools Available Online

In the volume of this book, I found it impossible to provide a complete set of all the customized tools in the *"Recruit the Best"* system.Therefore I have made available to you the following tools in complete downloadable files. Go to www.CanTheySell.com. There you will find the following tools that you can reproduce for your personal use.

- Matching Score Sheet
- Phone Screen Questionnaire
- Email Screen Questionnaire
- Initial Interview Questionnaire
- Reference Check Questionnaire
- Interview by Team Member Questionnaire
- In-depth Interview Questionnaire

These tools are available for purchase and download. Remember, when you purchase them, you can reproduce them only for your personal use. Reproduction for distribution to others is strictly prohibited and punishable by law. By obeying this law, you help me to continue to be productive in my efforts to serve others. If you wish to purchase a corporate distribution license, please contact me for details.

Other Recruiting Resources and Getting Connected through Social Networking Channels

For ongoing coaching, additional information and motivation in all activities related to sales, go to www.SalesManage.com. To order a CPQ, go to www.CraftProfiles.com. When you order a CPQ, I, or one of my highly trained staff, will give you personal assistance with your hiring challenges. Direct your salespeople to go to www.SalesActivities.com and sign up for a 30-day free trial. There they can learn to set goals and track their activities toward reaching their target income level. Start putting this system into action, then let me know how it is working for you. My personal email address is ssuggs@salesmanage.com, and I would love to hear from you. You can also read and comment at my two blogs, www.CanTheySell.com and www.SalesAcitivities.com/blog. Follow me on Twitter @Steve_Suggs, on Linkedin and on Facebook. Please join my Linkedin group "Can They Sell?" Join me, as we bring recruiting to a whole new level.

At YOUR Service,
Steve Suggs
Sales Manage Solutions, LLC

(1) *Craft Personality Questionnaire Interpretation Guide,* a PDF document, a Score Interpretation Guide designed for SHL clients who use the Craft Personality Questionnaire. SHL Group Ltd. is the publisher and copyright owner of the CPQ.

(2) The Basic Eight Traits, A Practitioner's Guide to the Administration and Interpretation of the Craft Personality Questionnaire®, Dr. Doug Waldo, SPHR, Larry L. Craft, EdD, Dr. Amanda Evans, PHR., DC Press, A division of CraftSystems, Inc., 1401 Manatee Avenue West, Suite 850, Bradenton, FL 34205. Copyright © 2006 by CraftSystems, Inc., Bradenton, Florida.

Part IV

Score Sheets and Checklist

Recruit the Best
Matching Score Sheet

Name: _____ Date: _____

Can they achieve the goals? Do they possess the competencies for the job? How do their personality traits match with what they must do? Do they have the most important attitudes and beliefs for your culture? How fast will they learn?

	GREAT		GOOD			MARGINAL			
SCORE	10	9	8	7	6	5	4	3	2	1
Attitude - product/sales										
Motivation – current/future										

	GREAT		GOOD			MARGINAL			
SCORE	10	9	8	7	6	5	4	3	2	1
Character Traits										
Honesty										
Concern for Others										
Work Ethic										
Responsible										

	GREAT		GOOD			MARGINAL			
SCORE	10	9	8	7	6	5	4	3	2	1
Personality Traits										
Social Drive – High										
Social Confidence – High										
Goal Orientation – High										
Need for Control - High										

	GREAT		GOOD			MARGINAL			
SCORE	10	9	8	7	6	5	4	3	2	1
Competencies Required										
Prospecting/Networking										
Setting/Holding Appntments										
Fact Finding										
Presenting Solutions										
Handling Objections										
Closing the Sale										

In-depth Interview Score: _____

Recruit the Best
Matching Score Sheet

Write in Evidence for (+) or against (-) Each

	+	-
Character Traits		
Concern for Others		
Honesty		
Hard Work Ethic		
Personally Responsible		

Personality Traits		
High Social Drive		
High Social Confidence		
High Goal Orientation		
High Need for Control		

	+	-
Competencies Required		
Prospecting/Networking		
Setting/Holding Appointments		
Fact Finding		
Presenting Solutions		
Handling Objections		
Closing the Sale		

Recruit the Best
Checklist

Name: _____ Date:_____

❏ 1. Review resume.

❏ 2. Screen by Phone – Use *Phone Screen Questionnaire.* If successful, go to next step.

❏ 3. Screen by Email – send "Thank you" email with these questions: **Date sent_____**
> *What do you think this job involves?*
> *What do you think it will take to be successful here?*
> *Tell me why I should consider you for this position?*
> *What specifically in your life do you want to change?*
> *How will being successful in this job help you with this change?*
>
> **Date Candidate Responded _____**

If successful, schedule face-to-face initial screening interview.
> **Date of Interview_____**

❏ 4. Email Initial Interview homework - Prior to the interview, email the candidate instructing them to go to the following Websites and review the information prior to the interview:

> To learn about our products and a career with us, go to: **www.ABCcorp.com**
> **Emailed on_____**

> Prior to Initial Interview, email the candidate to confirm the interview and make sure they have reviewed the Web pages. **Date confirmed_____**

❏ 5. Conduct Initial Face-to-Face Interview – Use *Initial Interview Questionnaire*

❏ 6. Ask for a list of 6 references – 2 previous bosses, 2 coworkers, 2 business people/former customers.

❏ 7. Call References using *Reference Check Questionnaire.*

❏ 8. *Administer the *Craft Personality Questionnaire (CPQ)* www.craftprofiles.com
> **Date CPQ Ordered_____**

If CPQ is strong, schedule In-depth Interview
> **Date of Interview_____**

❏ 9. Conduct In-depth Interview – Use *In-depth Interview Questionnaire*

❏ 10. Interview By Current Team – Use *Team Interview Questionnaire*

❏ 11. Fill out Matching Sheet

Many recruiters choose to administer the CPQ prior to the Initial Fact-to-Face Interview in step 5. They prefer to have the personality information available prior to the interview.